In
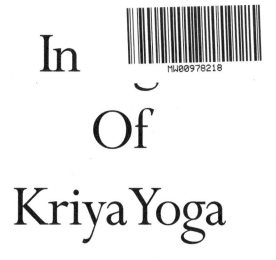
Of
Kriya Yoga

By

Rudra Shivananda

Alight Publications

2006

In Light of Kriya Yoga

By Rudra Shivananda

First Edition Published in July 2006

Alight Publications
PO Box 930
Union City, CA 94587

http://www.Alightbooks.com

ISBN 1-931833-13-3

Printed in the United States of America

Dedicated

to the

Eternal Light

That Guides

All of Us

In the Light of Kriya Yoga

Contents

A Note to the Reader

Part 1: The Light that Leads

Part 2: Pathways to the Light

Part 3: The Light that Shines

A Note to the Reader

The spiritual path is a long and difficult journey with many pitfalls and tempting detours. Moses had a pillar of cloud by day and a pillar of fire by night to guide him through the trackless desert and it still took him forty years.

When one goes on a long journey to a new land, it is helpful to consult a guidebook and a roadmap. A guidebook gives information about the places one will be passing through and useful hints on what to do and what to avoid. Frequently, there maybe lists of equipment to take and advice on the amount of money and resources needed. A roadmap provides the various routes that one can take to the desired destination as well as brief descriptions of monuments or signs that you can follow to ensure that one doesn't get lost.

Neither the guidebook nor the travel map will teach you how to drive a car – that is something you have to learn from a competent driving instructor. It is also necessary to obtain a license from the appropriate authority before one actually is allowed to operate the car.

I have provided both a guidebook and a roadmap for the *yogic* spiritual path. In it you will find straightforward, clear and penetrating explanations and insights into profound and perplexing subjects that concern every seeker on the path. This is not a detailed instructional book on *yogic* techniques or practices. I have written other books for instructional purposes which can be consulted if so desired.

In the first part of the present work, the Light that guides us on the path is variously described. It is difficult to travel in the dark, and some form of light is necessary to show the way. This Light can take many forms depending on our needs. Sometimes, the guiding light comes from an external teacher; sometimes it comes as inner guidance, from sacred scriptures or even as inspiring parables. The Light can manifest for us in good people and saints or in Self-Realized Masters and Perfected Beings. We should be ready to accept the manifestation of our evolutionary impulse towards the Divine in whatever form it comes.

In the second part of the text are descriptions of the various paths to reach Self-Realization, the first goal of spiritual evolution. Unlike a physical journey in which the various routes have different sign posts, rest-stops, detours and beautiful monuments, all the *yogic* spiritual paths share common signs and experiences, both positive and negative. Even though I have given them from the Kriya Yoga perspective and through the form of Patanjali's Eightfold path, these insights are applicable to all ways to the Truth of Self-Realization. There are helpful tips to progress faster on the journey, descriptions of obstacles to avoid and methods to overcome obstructions along the path.

The third part of this book is dedicated to elucidating various ways to enjoy and make the most of the journey. In it are helpful guides to using certain tools to enhance the life-experience. There are also descriptions of humans who have transformed into world teachers, or into perfected super-beings. However, the focus is on the means to live a happy life and being spiritual in this material world.

May these experiential insights be of benefit to the reader and practitioner. My inspiration flows continuously from my Master, Yogiraj Gurunath Siddhanath, from whom I have experienced greater and greater dimensions of the mysterious deathless Being called Babaji.

Enjoy the journey and may this small offering be a helpful companion to all sincere spiritual seekers.

Shiva-Gorakasha-Babaji

Yogiraj Gurunath Siddhanath

Rudra Shivananda

Part 1

The Light that Leads

1

The Light of Kriya

The undying light of the Divine is in each of us. No matter how we choose to live our lives, this light always shines within us and gives us illumination and inspiration. This light leads us back to our home and no matter how lost we think we are, the right path is always lit by the Divine with us.

When we make an effort on the spiritual path, this inner guidance will shine brighter and can lead us to realms beyond our imagination.

I will relate an experience which illustrates how subtly the light of the Divine can give us inner guidance. In fact, most of the time, we are unaware of this guidance and attribute to ourselves the inspiration that comes.

There is a story concerning Lord Shiva (the Eternal Lord of Yoga or that aspect of Divinity which helps those who yearn to re-unite with the Divine) that had troubled me since I first read it many years ago. It concerns the emergence of Ganesh, the divine aspect of wisdom. There are various versions, the most popular from the Puranas, goes like this:

> Once upon a time, Lord Shiva decided to go hunting with his followers. His wife, Parvati, stayed home and decided to take a bath – she was covered with the offerings from devotees all over earth! To guard her door so that no unauthorized person would disturb her, she took some of the holy paste from her body and fashioned a boy and breathed life into it – a son was thus born. Parvati instructed her new son to stop anyone trying to disturb her while she was enjoying her bath. So, the boy Ganesh obediently stood guard outside her door, holding a sharp sword.
>
> It so happened that Lord Shiva decided to return early and when He tried to enter His home, He was stopped by

this boy who refused to let Him in, even after the Lord had announced who He was. His infuriated devotees tried to force their way past Ganesh, but were repelled by the boy's power. Finally, Shiva became angry and cut of the boy's head with his trident.

Now, when Parvati found out what had happened to her son, she got really upset and could not be consoled. Finally, the Lord promised to restore the boy to life. However, the head of Ganesh had been thrown so far away, that it could no longer be found, and so Shiva asked his followers to bring back the head of the first dead creature they could find. They returned with the head of a newly died elephant, and so Shiva put it on the shoulders of the dead boy, and resuscitated the body. That was how the elephant-headed Divine aspect called Ganesh born.

There are many aspects of this story that bothered me:
· How could the omniscient Shiva not know who the boy was?
· How could the Supreme Yogi, the Lord of Self-Realization, get angry and resort to a violent act?
· Why didn't He just put the original head back on? In some versions, the head was stolen, but how could it be hidden from Shiva?

Of course, these stories are not meant to be taken literally, and are meant to illustrate some higher principles for the understanding of the readers. There are detailed explanations for the symbolism of Ganesh – that he is the symbol of "Om", the primordial sound of creation reverberating in the Universe to this day; how the side view of the elephant head, with its trunk was the shape of Om. However, this particular story made little sense to me when I read it, and this puzzling action of Shiva was not explained in other books or by oral tradition from yogis. It was just one of those inexplicable things. In my heart, I knew that the ancient story-tellers must have some deeper meaning in mind, but soon gave up on trying to puzzle it out.

I forgot about this unsatisfactory tale until one day, there was a discussion among some of my friends concerning Ganesh, and one of them related the above story, elucidating considerable mirth all around. Unfortunately, I could not really give a better explanation and had to suffice with the weak assertion that there was more to the story than is now understood – that the sages of old had some reason to relate such an apparently nonsensical story. There must be something instructional about it, but the key may have been lost, at least to us.

That same day, during my evening meditation, I asked Babaji, the immortal founder of Kriya Yoga, to give me the key to understanding the myth better. This is not as unusual as it sounds because all sincere practitioners of Kriya Yoga are guided by Babaji, even though He seldom appears physically to His devotees. There is always a strong astral and spiritual connection in those who have formed a relationship with Him.

However, Babaji is never predictable. In this instance, I felt that He had answered me but I could not access the information. He smiled and assured me that at the right moment, the answer would present itself. Through the years, I had learned not to argue with Him and so had to let go of my frustration.

A few months later, during a workshop that I was giving, a student asked me about Shiva and mentioned the infamous story of Ganesh. As I began to respond, Babaji's answer was revealed to me, and I spontaneously gave a detailed explanation that satisfied not only my students, but myself as well!

Briefly, the son of Parvati was fashioned from Matter only, since he was created by the Divine Mother from the dirt of Her body without the Spirit from the Divine Father. Therefore, the boy was an embodiment of ignorance and darkness. This ignorance is exemplified by the boy's inability to recognize his Divine Father. He stubbornly refused to accept the Spirit and clung to his delusion, even after Shiva's identity had been revealed. Shiva is the destroyer of the ego and in compassion, He "cut off the boy's head" removing the ego and ignorance, replacing it with the "head of an elephant" – the symbol of wisdom in India, infusing him with the Divine Spirit. Therefore, the boy had to be reborn as Ganesh. This act of Shiva is the transformation of Matter to Spirit! It is meant to teach us that wisdom comes from cutting off the ego born of ignorant matter.

I relate this simple story to illustrate that Babaji is the Light of Kriya. He illuminates our minds with His wisdom, driving out ignorance, just as a lamp brought into a dark room can make the darkness disappear. Each one of us can avail of His guidance – we only need to open ourselves up through the sincere practice of Self-Realization. I know my Divine light as Babaji, you may know this inner guidance by some other name. It is human to try to limit everything by giving a name, but the Divine is Nameless.

note: Babaji is the name given to the deathless founder of Kriya Yoga in the classic, Autobiogaphy of a Yogi by Paramhansa Yogananda. It indicates the great Being's wish to remain annonymous, as the name means revered elder and is also an epithet for the Ancient of Days.

Spiritual Evolution

We are undergoing a spiritual evolution, whether we know or not, and this evolution is our primary purpose on this plane of existence. What are we evolving towards? That is shown and demonstrated by the great beings such as a Christ, a Buddha or a Krishna, who have come among us as beacons of light for our evolutionary journey.

The question is whether there is anything we can do that will help accelerate the normal rate of spiritual evolution. The goal is the awakening of the higher human faculties and transformation in the structure as well as function of the human nervous system, hastening the evolution of humanity and consequential healing of physical, mental and emotional ills.

Our present state is only an intermediate stage, and not the ultimate in humanity's evolution. The suffering in the external world is a mirror of the internal pain and confusion in our consciousness. Only by evolving and healing our internal consciousness will the utopian ideal world of the "golden age" be actualized in the external world.

If we can jump over our finite mind, we can experience a new dimension of existence, expand the frontiers of our consciousness and enable the expression of the highest creative energies. In order to achieve this, we must transcend the limitations of the confined mind bounded by the stimuli of the five senses, not by escaping from it, but by achieving our highest potential, and redefining it, just as the Einsteinian Universe transcended the Newtonian Universe.

Each of us is a potential star! More than that, each of us is potentially Divine. The great sages have told us that we can hold galaxies in the palm of our hands. Such are the teachings of the Ancients. We've been brought up to reject such wild concepts. Wealth and position in society are now the desired goals to strive towards. In our hearts we feel the hollowness of realizing such "lofty" aspirations, but nonetheless, follow the prescribed rut - the path of least resistance.

Reality as perceived by the sages is much more glorious. The earth itself is star-dust, born from stellar debris, and is constantly evolving. From the earth we obtain our bodies, and from our star, the Sun, we receive our life, and our soul.

There is an impetus in earth matter to evolve. The physical aspects of evolution have now assumed the loftiness of Darwinian Gospel. Few dispute the evolution from single cell toward multi-cell organisms, from invertebrate to vertebrate, from reptiles to mammals. Although the real story is much more complex for scientific comfort and man's role as yet clouded by yawning gaps, it is a helpful analogy to the immensity that is spiritual evolution. The ancient masters of Yoga have always recognized and taught evolution. In fact, the goal of these ancient spiritual scientists was to accelerate the evolutionary process.

How did we get to this state where we need to evolve – how did this whole cycle get started? The greatest sages such as the Buddha have refused to answer such a question because in our present state of consciousness, it would be impossible to comprehend the answer.

The sages have taught that at some level we need to know that there is a process of involution called *nivritti marg* by which the One, infinite, indivisible Reality creates out of itself a world of multiplicity, divided and ignorant of the Divine Truth. Concurrently, there arises an evolutionary impulse called the *pravritti marg* by which these created forms struggle to survive, grow and rise in consciousness to manifest the Divine potential. Life then becomes a manifestation of spiritual reality and the evolution of life is an expression of the evolution of consciousness that the spirit undertakes for the delight of self-discovery and manifestation in the world of forms.

The progress of man in this cycle of evolution is facilitated by the law of Karma and the mechanism of reincarnation. Many of the riddles of life are unraveled by realizing these fundamental aspects of life. Karma is a spiritual law analogous to physical laws such as gravitation. It is based on causation – our current life and character are the outcome of our previous actions – this means not just our actions, speech and thoughts of this life, but of all our previous lives. For every action there is a reaction that is recorded and will become the driving force for future births.

The state of a "normal" human being is limited to body and superficial mental consciousness, and yet controlled by the vaster unknown depths of sub- and un- consciousnesses.

We are not aware that the "individual" body/mental consciousness is only one mode of a vaster framework of evolution to soul consciousness, universal consciousness and finally to naked and empty Being, from which all beings arise.

When human evolution advances to the highest level, the subconscious mind is cleared, ego is dissolved and super-consciousness is awakened. Even as ordinary human consciousness is light-years beyond animal consciousness, so super-consciousness is beyond the ordinary human intellect, logic and reasoning. There is a relationship between spiritual evolution and physical evolution. At the lowest level, most animals are driven by the instincts of the unconscious mind, while primates such as monkeys and apes, can function with habits and programmed conditioning. It is at the level of humanity that the consciousness ego personality comes into full play. Only in the Yogi is the super-conscious state operative, which can yet evolve further into the Cosmic Consciousness of Self-Realization.

When the highest level of evolution is not only isolated among a few exceptional individuals, but is prevalent in a society, then that society exists completely in harmony with Nature, beyond technology, religion and violence.

In order to understand the process of spiritual evolution and methods of accelerating the process, one must turn towards knowledge of the subtle body.

We are not just this body which can see, touch, taste, smell, and hear. A particularly useful *yogic* model assumes that we all possess five bodies. In addition to the physical body, which we can experience with our five senses, we also have an energy body, which functions with our energy interfaces and stores our basic life-force. A third body is where we store our emotional patterns and the potential energy which function in this mode of our manifestation. The mental body is where our mind functions, and is the storage for our mental patterns and associations, as well as for our mental energies. The fifth body is the causal body which is the seat of our soul and repository of our *karmic* patterns from the cause and effect relationships which we have set into play. When we die, only the causal body survives and can be reincarnated into a new physical body.

There are many *yogic* systems which give more or less bodies and use different names for them, but the basic underlying agreement is that we have more than just the visible body, but also a subtle body, with a hierarchy of seven energy centers called *chakras*.

These Energy Centers cannot be found by dissecting the physical body, but only through achieving higher states of consciousness. They are called wheels because of the circular movement of the energies that whirl in and out of them. For our initial visualization, they are balls of light. You will be able to feel their circular movement as you progress on the spiritual journey.

These Energy Centers are affected by changes in our internal states, as well as by external vibrations, such as thoughts, words, or actions of others. In the average person, these Centers are functioning sub-optimally, and are not harmonized with each other. As the health of the person is decreased through pollution and tension, the more out of tune these Centers become. They need to be harmonized and balanced for optimal health.

These are the seven energy centers:

Center 1: This is also called the Root Center, and is located at the base of the spine in the perineum and is the root and support of all the other centers. It is connected with the subtle element "earth" representing solidity, and therefore is closely related to the physical body. This is where the animal or unconscious mind is dominant.

Center 2: This is located two inches above the 1st Center along the spine, and is associated with the subtle element water, representing fluidity and movement. This is the center for the emotional body.

Center 3: This is located at the level of the navel, and is associated with the subtle element fire, representing transformation of energy. This center is closely related to the energy body.

Center 4: This is located at the spine at the heart level and is associated with the subtle element air, representing the mind and is the center of the mental body. This is the location where sub-consciousness gives way to normal consciousness.

Center 5: This is located at the throat and is associated with the subtle element ether, representing consciousness. This is the center for the causal or spiritual body, and is considered the seat of the soul. Here normal consciousness is dominant.

Center 6: This is located in the center of the head at the level just above the eyes, traditionally called the "third eye" and is the center for super-consciousness.

Center 7: this is located at the crown of the head and is associated with the Absolute or Transcendent Reality. Here is the center of Cosmic Consciousness.

The state of consciousness of the individuated person is the sum total of the states of the seven *chakras* in the subtle body. It is significant to understand that the seven *chakras* or energy centers we have described are in the energy body. However, there are similar *chakras* in all the other bodies and it is through their mutual vibrations that each body affects the others. This fact is not given in the *yogic* texts specifically, but can be experienced by all sincere practitioners.

There is an order of enlightened beings that quietly assists in the spiritual development of humanity over vast periods of time. These immortal sages work in the background to ensure the timely release and teaching of evolutionary practices according to the capacity of the more advanced souls of the period. Babaji is one such compassionate being who has toiled tirelessly for humanity, bestowing the science of Kriya Yoga, whenever it becomes possible for this highest spiritual science to be disseminated.

Kriya Yoga is a system focusing on the awakening of the *pranic* or life-force *chakras* in the Energy Body. The six main energy centers along the spine are the main concern for this path. Kundalini is the energy frozen at the base or first *chakra*, representing humanity's highest potential. The aim of these techniques is to awaken this Kundalini energy from a potential into a kinetic state, so that it pierces all the six energy centers, resulting in the achievement of super-consciousness. This also requires the dissolution of all the obstructions to higher states of consciousness.

This is simultaneously an ancient *yogic* path and a modern approach highly accessible to spiritual seekers. It has been popularized by Paramhansa Yogananda in the Autobiography of a Yogi and through his intense thirty year effort in the U.S.

Immortal Babaji has designated Kriya Yoga as the primary vehicle for spiritual evolution in these times. It is very well suited to enable a house-holder to achieve Self-realization as witnessed by its first two Masters in modern times - Lahiri Mahasaya and Sri Yukteswar. Lahiri

Mahasaya had children after being initiated by Babaji. There should not be a misunderstanding from the fact that Yogananda was a renunciate that Kriya Yoga is for those who want to leave the world. Quite the contrary – it is the best system for the yogi engaged in worldly activities.

Over time, there have arisen many yogic paths and even a variety of Kriya Yogas. Whichever Kriya system is practiced, the goal is the evolution from ego to spiritual equality or One-ness. It is the development from fear and desire to self-knowledge and humility. It is the evolution from dissipation to self-discipline, from ignorance to knowledge, falsehood to truth, and from pain of existence to delight of existence.

The process we see here is the same process that occurs at the social, psychological and spiritual levels. The whole world is only the Divine involved in matter, in ignorance, in prejudice, selfishness, falsehood etc. It is only the Divine, nothing else.

The contacts that come to us from life have only one purpose, to awaken the higher consciousness so we can discover the hidden Godhead and it can more fully manifest on the surface. We may not discover the full Divinity, but we can discover more of the latent potential of our own inner being, which is a portion and expression of that Divinity. We can give up falsehood, jealousy, meanness, and the like. We can discover our greater capacities and higher nature and rise up to be fully human.

In order to understand the evolution fully, we must understand the essential role and process of the involution. The involution provides the necessary foundation and circumstances for the evolution. All that we perceive as unconsciousness, opposition, obstacle, resistance, hostility and perversity—in others, the life around us and even in ourselves—are products of the involution that play essential roles in the emergence of positive characteristics and accomplished capacities in the evolution. Involution is the essential basis for the evolution. Mind has involved in body because the ignorance and limitation of matter is essential for the evolution of life and mind in matter. We can see it in life. Each difficult problem that arises for us because of an involved consciousness becomes a stimulus for our progress, without which we could not evolve.

To evolve, we must recognize and affirm the values of goodness and generosity and reject our sense of self-importance or ego. Through this process, the hidden consciousness emerges in strength and joy, and we evolve from unconsciousness to super-consciousness, from vanity to humility.

Falsehood is inverted or involved Truth. It is a power of truth distorted and perverted by ignorance and ego. The evolution of consciousness is an evolution of consciousness out of unconsciousness, truth out of falsehood. As a power of truth, it is itself an instrument of the evolution. It is a prior state of involution, which is an essential condition and means for the evolution. The role of falsehood in others is to help us shed our own falsehood. Although we often regard a small lie as necessary or convenient to promote our aims, when opportunities open up at a higher level, the introduction of falsehood or the inability to totally eliminate it can only limit, postpone or cancel that higher opportunity to spiritual evolution.

Individuals act from the reactive patterns of their *karmic* make-up. But given the character, each individual is capable of more than one type of response to any situation. In other words, results of actions are a product not only of human character but also of human choice. Human consciousness consists of multiple layers or levels ranging from the pure physical to the pure mental and to spiritual levels beyond mind. Each individual being possesses all these levels, developed in varying degrees. Each individual is capable of acting from any of these levels, but normally has a characteristic plane of action - a maximum plane reached at the most creative moments and a minimum level that is reached at times of extreme crisis. In any specific action, an individual may choose to express qualities of one or several of these levels. We can choose to evolve and participate further in the involution or not.

We are the sum of our choices, at every moment. This responsibility is both comforting and disquieting, but it is our responsibility.

We cannot blame the Divine for our personal suffering and we cannot lay blame on the Divine for all the suffering in the world. We, as human beings, are collectively responsible.
Spiritual evolution is the key to individual peace and to social harmony – a world of love and contentment – a place of divine joy. Let us take the personal responsibility to evolve for the sake of all humanity.

Let us take up the call of the vedic sages as they call out:

O Lord please lead me from the unreal to the real.
Lead me from darkness to light.
Lead me from death to immortality.
May there be peace, peace, and perfect peace.

The True Kriya Yoga

There are many different organizations, yogic schools, and individuals teaching many varieties of practices and all claiming to be guardians of the "true Kriya Yoga." This can be confusing to the sincere seeker.

Is there really a true Kriya Yoga? The good news is that most of those groups are keepers of the flame of Kriya. Even though they may teach different techniques or different varieties of similar techniques, many have legitimate claims through their lineages and the common factors that distinguish Kriya Yoga from other types of yoga.

Why then are there so many varieties? The answer lies in the effectiveness of these techniques to provide Self-Realization. Over the last one hundred and forty years, there have been a number of Yogic Masters who have achieved their spiritual evolution through Kriya Yoga, and they have incorporated, simplified, developed and modified what they had learned to suit the needs of their own disciples. It is important to understand that only Masters may modify or evolve what has been passed on down to them because only they can ensure that the effectiveness of the techniques is not diminished.

However, no matter how the Masters have altered Kriya Yoga, there are certain features that will remain constant. What then are these distinguishing marks? It is not necessary to invoke oral tradition to determine these features. They have been plainly given to us in two ancient yogic texts and one more contemporary spiritual classic. The three texts that illuminate Kriya Yoga are: Bhagavad Gita, Patanjali's Yoga Sutras and Yogananda's Autobiography of a Yogi.

Through the transmission of these texts, it is clear that the following are the distinguishing marks of Kriya Yoga:

1. It originates with Babaji, the mysterious immortal whose presence is whispered throughout the length and breadth of the

Himalayas. It is said that Lord Krishna learned Kriya Yoga from Shiva-Babaji, perhaps circa 3000 BCE. During the dark age of 2400 years between 600 BCE and 1800 CE, only very exceptional sages such the Siddha Patanjali could even learn this yoga. As humanity's consciousness once more became ready, the Light of Kriya initiated blessed Lahiri Mahasaya and once more accelerated the wheel of spiritual evolution. All true Kriya Yoga will claim lineage to Babaji.

2. The control and expansion of life-force energy or *prana* is an essential part of the practice. Lord Krishna says, "Kriya Yoga is the offering of the outgoing to the incoming breath." Here He is referring not just to the common breath, but to the *prana* permeating the cosmos and within the human body. Patanjali emphasized that *tapas* or the building of the inner fire by effort was a mark of Kriya Yoga. Fire is built by rubbing two sticks together and in a similar way, the internal fire is built through the practice of cycling the incoming life-force called *prana* and the outgoing life-force called *apana*. This is the *prana-apana yagna* or internal fire-ceremony. Yogananda has very clearly stated that the *kriya pranayama* is a natural scientific breath that rejuvenates the body cells and magnetizes the spine, the conduit of spiritual evolution. Therefore, spinal breathing is an essential element of Kriya Yoga. In addition, he warns us that, "Kriya Yoga has nothing in common with unscientific breathing exercises. Their attempts to forcibly hold breath in the lungs is not only unnatural but decidedly unpleasant."

3. A sense of Devotion is required, because Kriya Yoga is characterized as an "offering," and techniques done mechanically will not be effective. A science of Self-Realization has as one of its key ingredients, a sense of the Divine as the True Self. Patanjali emphasized this alignment with the True Self as i*svara pranidhana* or surrender to one's true nature. Lord Krishna has given the first steps toward devotion and

surrender to the Divine by instructing us to offer all the fruits of our actions, including that of our spiritual practice, at the feet of the Divine. Be a Karma Yogi – work with love for the Lord as a matter of duty without a selfish desire for the fruits or any attachment to the results – practicing *nishkama karma* yoga is true devotion.

4. Introspection and self-study is a key to higher consciousness and so *svadyaya* is required. This can include the study of authoritative texts or meeting with sages, but will invariably lead to a course of meditation or *dhyana*. A sense of awareness is necessary to reach higher consciousness. Awareness passes through various stages – in the beginning it can be humiliating and depressing, as we become more aware of our thoughts, words and deeds; then progress to joy in the expansion of the soul as it aligns closer to the Divine; finally constant awareness leads to constant bliss.

5. Kriya Yoga is for the spiritual evolution of the householder – this has been made clear to Lahiri Mahasaya by Babaji. Lahiri Baba was himself a householder and had children even after being initiated by his immortal Master. Many of his disciples were family men with jobs and responsibilities. Among them was Shri Yukteswar, who was married, but later became a renunciate Swami, after the death of his wife. The confusion that has arisen concerning the identification with a religious order and practicing Kriya Yoga was caused by the fact that Yogananda chose to become a renunciate due to his single-minded devotion to the Divine and because of the demands of his mission to spread Kriya Yoga in the West. Yogananda has become the symbol of Kriya Yoga to many, and rightly so, for his many achievements. However, the fact that Yogananda as well as a number of Shri Yukteswar's disciples belonged to a Swami order, has no material bearing on Kriya Yoga.

It is up to each person drawn to Babaji and to Kriya Yoga to choose
the variety that best suits his or her temperament. Each of us has come
to this world with different set of burdens and challenges as well as
opportunities. Yogananda is reputed to have said that "many paths
lead to the top of the mountain, but once reached, the view is the
same." May your choice of Kriya alternatives light up you life, and
may you reach the mountain top expeditiously. As Lord Krishna said
to Arjuna, "The path of Self-Realization and the path of ego-ignorance
are thought to be the two eternal paths of the world. The latter leads to
rebirth while the former to liberation. Knowing these two paths, O
Arjuna, a yogi is not bewildered in any way. Therefore, be steadfast in
yoga at all times."

Self-Realization

How does one recognize someone who has achieved Self-Realization? How does such a one act? This is an important question for all of us and was asked by Arjuna in the Bhagavadgita, more than five-thousand years ago.

After all, the examples from our spiritual history give little guidance – many who achieved Self-Realization were married people or even householders with family responsibilities and social duties, while others were ascetic renunciates meditating in caves. What are the common features or marks which distinguish them from those who have not achieved Self-Realization?

An unrealized person is driven by desires, never contented, always looking for fresh satisfaction. These desires are manifested from latent impulses called *samskaras* which are linked into habit patterns called *vasanas*. These samskaras and vasanas are the results of our past actions – our karma from past lives.

The Self-Realized have wiped clean their conditions of samskaras and vasanas – free from desires of any kind. Therefore Lord Krishna tells Arjuna:

> *When a man completely casts off all the desires of the mind, his Self finding satisfaction in Itself alone, then he is called a man of Self-Realization. He who is not perturbed by adversity, who does not long for happiness, who is free from attachment, fear and wrath, is called a sage of Self-Realization.*
> Bhagavadgita: 2.55 and 2.56

One who is Self-Realized has no need to try to find futile fulfillment in acquiring, possessing or indulging in material pleasures or objects. Contentment arises from awakening to reality, to unconditioned super-consciousness.

The unrealized person is driven by vasanas to acquire possessions or pleasures, to which he becomes attached. Fear then arises when the possibility of losing that to which there is attachment. When something is actually lost, anger arises.

Without any vasanas, the Self-Realized is not subject to the cycle of attachment, fear and anger:

> *He who is not attached to anything, who neither rejoices nor is vexed when he obtains good or evil – his wisdom is firmly fixed.*
>
> Bhagavadgita: 2:57

The unrealized are driven by their ego to evaluate the world around them and categorize everything into either good or evil, to them. This causes them to praise those who give them "good" and to blame those who cause "evil" to befall them.

The Realized have no ego and do not evaluate objects or people as good or evil. They accept things as they are, as natural happenings and are not affected in any way:

> *That man who lives completely free from desires, without longing, devoid of the senses of "I" and "mine," attains peace.*

Unfortunately it is not easy to distinguish someone who is truly Self-Realized and someone who is merely trying to be so or even someone who is only pretending, by means of their outward words or deeds. Of course, one who has discovered his true Self will know another one regardless of outward actions or speech. However, for those still on the path, it may require longer periods of observation, verification from a reliable source and some degree of spiritual discernment.

Let us consider an example to illustrate this challenge - a sage who has realized his true Self will not be subject to ego and karmic patternings and will love and help even those who have harmed them:

An old man, a true yogi, used to go to a village to beg for food and was habitually taunted and hurt by young rascals throwing stones at him. He would take no offense and would smile and say loving words to them, even though his body was bleeding. One day, as he entered the village, the mother of his chief tormentor fell down before him and begged him to see the boy, who had been stricken with a deadly disease. Without hesitation or thought, he went and healed the rascal. If another sadhu (someone practicing a sadhana or yogic practice) had been subjected to the same experience, he would harbor some degree of animosity, but his ego would reason that as someone aspiring to wisdom, he should act kindly towards the boy – that is there would a mental tug-of-war between his joy that the Divine had punished his tormentor and his desire to act like a yogi would. This mental exercise might last only a short few seconds, but he would decide to go and heal the boy eventually. The difference between the true yogi and the sadhu would be only a matter of a few seconds, which might not be perceptible to others!

Another misconception often encountered is the confusion about the displays of paranormal or super powers and the state of Realization. Patanjali has enumerated the *siddhis* or powers of the true yogi in his Yoga Sutras, but they are not meant to be displayed frivolously. Yogis have used their powers to heal those that needed healing according to the will of the Divine, or to destroy ignorance and evil. There have also been many *sadhus* who have been seduced by the powers that they have acquired through their practices and have abandoned the goal of Self-Realization. These backsliding *sadhus* display and use their powers for personal benefit, sometimes pretending to do so for others, causing confusion in the minds of the masses.

A true yogi has surrendered to the Divine Will, and does not act individually to impress others or to benefit someone because of a financial arrangement. If such a one should ever use spiritual powers, it would be because it is in accordance to the Divine Will. A true yogi cannot be taunted or incentivized to contravene the natural enfoldment of spirituality. However many amazing events can occur in their presence or by their grace – their super-conscious state of awareness enable miracles to occur.

Therefore, it is not simple to differentiate a true yogi and someone who has acquired paranormal powers. The sincere seeker should be cautious in the face of "spiritual powers," and need to give greater weight to the wisdom and non-attachment that are the true marks of the Self-Realized.

Do not abandon common sense even in spiritual matters and cultivate patience and a discriminative nature. In this way, you will find the true yogi.

The Perfected One – the Siddha

According to yogic tradition, attainment of Self-Realization is not the end of the spiritual quest. After realization of one's true Self, there are still deeper and deeper realizations and vaster and vaster states of consciousness to be attained beyond the super-conscious. All subtle barriers to complete unity with the Divine have to be overcome. The states of Self-Realization have to be stabilized through experiences of samadhi (blissful state of unity consciousness) until it becomes constant and continuous.

An understanding of the goal is essential so that we do not get distracted by side paths or mistake lesser outposts as the final destination.

Patanjali, in his Yoga Sutras, has applauded the Siddhas as "Perfected Beings", beyond the yoga and yogic states which he is presenting. A yogi by focusing all the light in his head will achieve the vision of the Siddhas:

> *From perfect discipline of the light in the head, one gets a vision of the perfected beings (Siddhas).*
> Yoga Sutras 3.32

There is confusion among many people that the Siddhas are those who possess *siddhis* or paranormal powers. This is not true. The Siddhas are those who have gone beyond the *siddhis*, which are merely the by-products of their attainment. There are many minor *siddhis* or psychic powers which come to those on the spiritual path and these can even be developed by the worldly ones who seek to use them for materialistic gains.

Patanjali and other Masters have enumerated eight maya *siddhis*, showing power over the illusionary world of manifestation. These include becoming as small as an atom and as large as the universe, weightlessness, awareness extended throughout the universe, power to enter another body, control of phenomena, bring life to the dead and wish-fulfillment.

However, Patanjali has also stated that, "these attainments are obstacles to cognitive absorption but are accomplishments in the waking state." (3.37) For normal people, these psyhic powers are useful to getting things done in the material world, but they become impediments to going into higher super-conscious states that are beyond the cause and effect and time-space continuum.

The goal of Patanjali's Yoga is the union of jiva or the individualized soul with Ishwara, God manifest. Self-Realization is attained when the mental fluctuations cease and the Self alone remains in the state of Kaivalya. This is achieved through the surrender to the personal manifestation of the Divine called Ishwara. Patanjali expounded individual effort and practice.

There is a great Himalayan Nath Siddha called Sundernath, who when teaching in South India, entered the body of a dead cow-herd and became known as Siddhar Tirumoolar. For the benefit of the Tamil people, he wrote the classic yogic treatise called Tirumandiram, in which he has provided us with a detailed and authoritative definition of a Siddha:

> 497.
> *they who are of five malas rid*
> *themselves Siva become;*
> *they blemishless become,*
> *they become Siddhas,*
> *attain state of Mukti finale,*
> *they uproot Jiva's bondage,*
> *end cycle of births;*
> *they alone are,*
> *who truth of peerless Tattvas realised.*

Therefore, a Siddha has attained final liberation or *mukti*, such that the jiva or individualized soul is no longer subject to rebirth. There is freedom from the five primal fetters or *malas*: egoity, world illusion, law of karma, desires, and ignorance. The goal of Tirumoolar's Yoga is the union of jiva with Shiva, the Divine Lord, and so all impurities must be destroyed.

Liberation comes in different varieties, since it is the liberation from the cycle of birth and death. There are at least four types of liberations that are assumed by Tirumoolar, since a Siddha is one who has given up or passed beyond the three other liberations or muktis:

1. Salokya Mukti – liberation as the Lord's servant
2. Samipya Mukti – liberation as the Lord's child
3. Sarupya Mukti – liberation as the Lord's friend

The Siddha has achieved the fourth type of Sayujya Mukti – liberation through complete union with the Lord!

2525
they abandoned muktis three as vain;
they dispelled enticing darkness of Pasa,
they rid themselves of anava'
they transcended "I" and "mine" consciousness,
they in constancy remained,
they, verily are Siva Siddhas.

The Self-Realized yogi who has set his heart on Sayujya Mukti, is empowered to become a Siddha through the Guru's grace with the *abhiseheka*, or the fourth and final initiation. This is not normally given in the material world but in the higher planes of unity consciousness, when the yogi is ready.

A yogi who has attained the eight *siddhis* or divine powers then passes through the seventh *chakra* or energy center on the top of the head. In the Tirumandiram, the seventh *chakra* is an eight-petalled lotus, in which the eight gods guard the eight directions, to reach Lord Shiva. Again, the *siddhis* come to the yogi but the goal is the attainment of union with the Divine in the realm beyond time-space called Para Loka:

671.
they are Siddhas
who together with siddhis eight
attain the Divine;
they reach Para Loka
and within them vision the dear Lord
then they reach him true
going beyond the boundaries eight.

The practice of a Siddha may vary, but the path to perfection is mapped out as follows:
  1. vision of Shiva's world – the divine light
  2. realization of the divine sound
  3. realization of Sat-Chit-Ananda (Being, Consciousness, Bliss)
  4. mastery of the 36 principles of creation or 36 Tattvas

125.
Siddhas they that Siva's world visioned,
Nada and Nadanta deep in them realised,
The Eternal, the Pure, reposing in Bliss unalloyed,
Thirty and six the steps to Liberation leading.

The *tattvas* are the universal categories or principles that are responsible for the unmanifest and manifest, the noumena and the phenomena. In the model of the Samkhya philosophy which forms one of the base of Yoga Philosophy, there are only twenty-five *tattvas* ending with Purusha or the cosmic soul, while for a Siddha there are 36 Tattvas, ending with Shiva:

Shiva, Shakti, Sadashiva, Iswara, Shuddhavidya, Maya Tattva, The Five Limitations, Purusha, Prakritti, buddhi, ahamkara, manas, five sense organs, five action organs, five subtle elements, and five gross elements.

These are like thirty-six steps, each one or grouping is dependent on the previous, and which together are the basic constituents of all creation. The Siddha masters each until he unites with Shiva and Shakti. The cycle of creation flows downward from Shiva to the five gross elements, while the cycle of return flows upstream and requires great effort and practice.

The Kriya Master, Sri Yukteswar, in his Holy Science has also provided us with a definition of a Siddha , as a yogi who has merged with the cosmic hum of the universe, the nadanta, achieving divinity, passing beyond the seven chakras:

He progresses in godliness, hears the holy Aum sound and becomes a Siddha or divine personage.

Then he perceives the manifestations of Spirit, and passes through the seven Patala Lokas (or centers in the spine), beholding the seven rishis.

The goal of Sri Yukteswar's Kriya Yoga is the union of the self with God as Sat-Chit-Ananda i.e.Being-Consciousness-Bliss.

The Siddhas served as beacons of light during their lifetimes. Moreover, many of them transformed their perishable bodies into immortal bodies of light and have remained on Earth for generations, to guide the spiritual evolution of humanity. Their leader is Babaji.

Note: the quotes from the Tirumandirum are from the translation by Dr. B. Natarajan.

Who is a Guru and do we need one?

The subject of the Guru or spiritual guide has always been contentious and the recent negative experiences among both Western and Eastern spiritual aspirants is nothing new. There has been rhetoric for and against the role of the Guru for many centuries even in India and the need for a Guru has from time to time been questioned, but always re-affirmed by the great yogis. However, there have been grave misunderstandings about the Guru and this ignorance has been largely responsible for the anti-Guru movement.

Let us examine the role of the Guru - what qualifications are required to take on such a duty, and whether we need one on the path.

It is not necessary to rely on the words of sages to affirm the need for a Guru. This is evident from all aspects of our lives – we have teachers from cradle to grave, helping us to learn everything we want or not. We do not generally believe that we can learn music, art, mathematics, engineering, martial arts, cooking, physics, flower-arrangement, computer skills etc., without the help of someone skilled in those areas. Is there any basis to believe that we can learn to achieve Self-Realization and cross the oceans of suffering without someone who has the knowledge and/or experience of achieving the desired goal?

There have been suggestions that the character of the Western culture may not be able to tolerate the Guru and that it does not fit the individualistic mentality here. What is lacking in the West is a lack of perspective and understanding their own history – it was less than two hundred years ago in all of Europe and USA where the Master/ Apprentice system was the principal manner by which someone learned a trade. It was only in comparatively recent times that mass education has replaced the apprentice system in which the apprentice serves the Master and after years of hard work becomes a journeyman, eventually to acquire the title of Master.

There is no difference in the karmic bonds that propel people eastern or western into suffering. Self-Realization is the cure, and the Guru is the doctor:

> *What is needed is a Guru, a Savior, who will awaken us to bhakti (devotion) and to perceptions of Truth.*
> Kaivalya Darsanam 1.17

The misunderstandings about who a Guru is and what he/she can do has been in part due to the ignorance of the tradition and also to the tendency among some spiritual teachers to take advantage of the ignorance.

It is necessary to heed the words of Lord Shiva, the lord of all yoga:

> *O Goddess, there are many gurus on earth who do not give the "Self," but in all the worlds, it is hard to find the Guru who reveals the "Self."*
>
> *Many are the gurus who rob the disciple of his wealth, but rare is the Guru who removes the disciple's afflictions.*
> *He is the Sat-Guru from whose contact there flows the supreme bliss (ananda.) The intelligent man should choose such a one as his Guru and none other.*

Ideally, a Guru is one who has achieved Self-Realization and therefore is bereft of ego and desires. Such a one can reveal the "Self" to the student. Finding such a Guru is not easy, for as Lord Shiva says, there are very few of them.

On the other hand, there are very few disciples who are prepared for the highest type of Guru. Students think a lot about the qualification of the Guru, but seldom review their own preparedness. Depending on their state of evolution, lesser teachers have to be relied on by most seekers. One should show respect for any being who can help us along the path. The yogis have observed that the student gets the teacher they deserve, but they also assured us that when the disciple is ready, the Guru will appear.

The spiritual seeker should do their best to verify the qualities of their spiritual guide, even if it may take years of observation. Unfortunately, such powers of discrimination are found in few seekers.

From a Guru's viewpoint, there are many students but few qualified disciples. How can one become ready? In the words of Shri Yukteswar, the Kriya Master:

One who cultivates the heart's natural love obtains the guidance of a Guru, and starts his sadhana (path of spiritual discipline.) He becomes a pravartaka, an initiate. By the practice of Yama and Niyama, the eight meannesses of the human heart disappear and virtue arises. Man thus becomes a sadhaka, a true disciple, fit to attain salvation.

Kaivalya Darsanam 4.6-7

It is seen that initiation by a Master is only the first step – it is then incumbent upon the initiate to practice the self-restraints called yama and the positive attitudes of niyama, in order to become fit to be a disciple. Students mistake the initiation as discipleship – many Western students of Masters claim to be disciples because they have been initiated into some practice, but that is not proper.

After one has verified the authenticity of the Guru, one should follow the Guru's instructions to develop moral courage, faith and love. Moral courage is necessary to overcome the obstacles caused by the ego, faith is necessary to stay the course and love is necessary to know we are not alone in the journey.

The role of the Guru has been changed from time to time according to humanity's general state of consciousness. In the vedic times, the Guru

30

is one who has realized the Truth and can communicate the Truth to the prepared. During the last two thousand years of the materialistic age, the quality of the prospective student has degenerated to the state where what used to be preparatory states have become advanced! During the last thousand years especially, with the dominance of Bhakti (yoga of devotion), the Guru has taken on the role of God. This would seem like a natural development, as the Guru should be one with the Divine, and so to be as close to the Divine as the normal person is likely to find. However, the Indian penchant for hyperbole used to glorify the Guru can easily be misunderstood and taken too literally. One should not mistake the finger pointing to the Moon as representing the Moon. One should not even mistake the reflection of the Moon in the lake for the Moon itself.

The Satguru shows the Divine and can lead the sincere towards Divinity.
Kaivlaya Darsanam 16-17

One of the distinctive ways that the Satguru can lead the sincere towards the Divine has been demonstrated and explained by my Master, Yogiraj Siddhanath as follows:

So the true Master should not only be in a state of Divine Consciousness and still awareness, but he must also be able to transfer and give unto receptive disciples this Divine Consciousness, this experience of his still Soul, (which I've called Shivapat.)
Wings to Freedom, P. 282

There is a misunderstanding that the disciple has to blindly obey the Guru, no matter what. Let us consider a great Guru – God Himself as the Avatar Lord Krishna. In the Bhagavad Gita, Lord Krishna encourages, counsels, and uses many ways to convince his disciple

Arjuna to take courage and defeat his internal enemies. Lord Krishna did not command it, not force it upon Arjuna. A Satguru does not command, force or intimidate his disciple. The Satguru is the embodiment of Love.

Another common mistake is to think that a Satguru is the Guru for everyone. This is seldom true. Even World Teachers whose teachings can influence many peoples for generations may have few true disciples. A person drawn towards the practice of devotion or *bhakti* may meet a Jnana Guru (a Satguru who leads to Divinity by the yoga of knowledge) and will not take such a Master. Students are drawn to teachers or teachings to which their karma predisposes them. Of course, it is possible to overcome programming, but that in itself is a spiritual battle, and it may be better to conserve one's strength to follow a teacher whose teachings can help the student faster.

It is worth mentioning that the popularity of a spiritual teacher does not necessarily indicate high attainment. Just as in ordinary activities, the masses are drawn to lower energies which they can capacitate and are not attracted to the highest. The Satguru may have very few disciples, if any!

Let the seeker humbly learn from everyone they meet on the path and prepare for the Guru.

My Master

Maya the mortal binds
Only a play the yogi finds
Death's claws in mortal hearts
Into nectar by siddha arts

No institution for liberation
No dogma cage nor fancy stage
No ochre robes nor color strobes
No ego balm nor actor's calm

A thousand life-times of tears
My soul cry finally He hears
In darkness a light, Yogiraj appears
Liberate me from countless fears

True yogi needs no external tools
True yogi one's body the only school
True Guru the only guiding light
Ignorant ego forces for to fight

Shiva-Shakti unparalled gift
Great Seal kundalini to lift
Five-pointed star to light the way
Cosmic hum leads home to stay

Sat-Gurunath Supreme
Wakes me from my dream
Drops drip from nectar well
Saves soul from karmic hell

In Light of Kriya Yoga

Soul bliss in third-eye sight
Pouring life Surya heaven's Light
On Earth Gurunath's lion might
In my heart Babaji's guiding light

Breathing through my breath
Thinking through my thoughts
In thy light I become aware
Grace saves from karmic snare

Clear light of no mind
O how rare to find!
Poetical verses I have none
Siddhanath you are the Sun.

Inner Guidance

A common pitfall encountered among spiritual seekers is the premature reliance on inner guidance and the consequent neglect of self-development or readiness to follow an external teacher or Master. Of course, the other side of the coin is the total reliance on the external Guru and the neglect to call on the Inner Guide when it becomes appropriate.

Both types of behavior are common because the mind is conditioned towards either/or situations and take comfort in black and white responses. On the path towards Self-Realization, binary logic has to be discarded.

The rationale for following inner guidance is sound. After all, we all have the Divine spark within us. However, it is often the ego which makes us think that in our present confused mind-state that it is possible to distinguish inner guidance from our subconscious outpourings. It is the ego that fears the discipline of following an external Teacher, the bridge between the objective and subjective. It is comforting but dangerous to rely on the subjective, especially in the beginning stages of the path.

On the development before inner guidance, the sage Patanjali has authoritatively stated:

> From the practice of the different parts of yoga, after the destruction of impurity, spiritual illumination arises that develops into awareness of reality.
>
> Yoga Sutras 2.28

Therefore, only after the sincere practice of the techniques of yoga can one expect to tune into the true Inner Guide. Until then, one should humbly learn from whoever has been sent by the Divine to guide us externally.

This does not mean that the practitioner should blindly follow his external guide, of whatever spiritual level he or she may be, and be fearful of following their own guidance. Yoga is not a religion - it is a science of Self-Realization. When the Inner Guide appears, then we must place ourselves in His grace. There is never any conflict between a Satguru or Master and the Inner Guide.

Again, Patanjali has described the Inner Guide as follows, "Being unconditioned by time, Ishvara is Teacher even of the ancient." (Yoga Sutras 1.26)

Ishwar is the Lord who is the unseen guide residing in our hearts.

Another description is given by Upamanyu in the epic Mahabharata, "Mahadeva, You impart instruction in utter silence. You observe the vow of equanimity for you instruct in silence."

Here, Lord Shiva is the Inner Guru who imparts liberation in silence. The form of Lord Shiva that is invoked as the Inner Guide is called Dakshinamurti. The following is a further description of this enigmatic Being:

How wonderful! Under a fig tree sits the youthful Teacher among aged disciples. The Teacher remains silent and yet the disciples are enlightened.
Dakshinamurti Upanishad

It is not possible to impart the truth of Absolute Knowledge through language, only through direct experience, in silence. Silence is the ultimate Divine Grace – it is what we all crave for in our souls.

Even those who have not sufficiently developed advanced states of consciousness where Dakshinamurti can lead them, have utilized external aids for connecting to some aspect of the inner guidance. Such techniques as the use of pendulums, muscle testing, tarot cards etc. serve as makeshift means to get connected to higher states of consciousness. However, there is always the danger that the ego or the sub-conscious desires may interfere with the guidance.

The yogic method is for direct intuition and the factors involved are:
· purification of the mind to develop the unimpeded pathways to direct intuition
· courage to follow guidance
· discrimination to separate true guidance from ego-mind play

A word of caution is in order for those who are still under the sway of their ego or subconscious programs (and after all, who isn't?) Under no circumstances would your inner guidance counsel violence against yourself or others. Truth (*satya*) and *ahimsa* (non-violence) are valuable yardsticks to guide our behavior, whether with external guides or the Inner Guide.

Ascent to Jwala Mukhi

It is always fortunate to be able to visit spiritual centers where great Masters have done their tapas or spiritual work for humanity. It is doubly auspicious to be able to make the visit in the presence of a living Master as well. This was the case some years ago when in I had the opportunity to participate on a pilgrimage with the Nath Master Gurunath.

One of the key spiritual centers which Gurunath led us to experience with him during the remarkable pilgrimage was Jwalaji, at the site of an ancient extinct volcano. This site is double treasured because it is both a Temple of the Divine Mother, as well as a Temple for Babaji Gorakhnath, the divine immortal.

We reached the sacred site in the early evening and sat down outside the temple where a group of pilgrims had gathered around three devotees who were chanting to the Divine Mother for deliverance from suffering. We joined in as their rhythmic drumming and chanting was very pleasing and soon mesmerizing as well.

Jwalaji is where, in the beginning, the Goddess energy manifested her Vak or Divine Voice in the form of flames. Vak is the essence of the Vedas, and is divine wisdom and knowledge. Devotees in constant and reverent procession file past at the appointed times when the temple gates are opened and they can obtain the darshan or divine grace of these living flames which appear in seven niches or crevices around the ancient walls. In spite of all the jostling crowds and the constant noise, it is an incredibly peaceful and centering experience. Great rulers of India have worshipped the Mother at Jwalaji and the current Golden Dome above the temple was an offering from Maharaja Ranjit Singh, the great ruler of Punjab during the early part of the 19th century

Behind and above the Goddess Temple is the edifice of the Gorakhnath Temple. This was built around a small space called the Gorakh Dhibi where during the years around 1000 AD, Shiva-Gorakhsha-Babaji spent some time meditating to purify and stabilize the region. There is a community of Kanphata Nath Yogis, some quite young, with their large earrings in their split ears (this is done to stimulate certain spiritual nadis or spiritual currents in the body.) A few of the pilgrims had unique experiences in meeting and talking with these dedicated spiritual practitioners of a similar lineage to ours.

One morning, I decided to go to the temple early in the morning. We were staying at a hermitage outside the village. While I walked through the deserted streets in the calm of dawn, heading towards the hill on which the temple was situated, there was a spring in my steps and a steadiness in my heart.

I walked past the deserted and shuttered shops, and just as I reached the incline that began the ascent towards the temple gates, a long-haired and bearded *sadhu* in flowing robes appeared from the side. He smiled and asked me what I wanted. I replied that I didn't want anything, and was just going up early to sit for meditation. He nodded, but once more asked me what I wanted.

From my past experience, itinerant yogis are generally looking to give their blessings and would expect some offering of money in exchange. I reached into my pocket and came up with a five hundred rupee note (a lot of money at that time), but he only shook his head and asked me what I wanted. Rather surprised by his refusal of the money, I looked carefully at him and was struck by his radiant face and unblinking magnetic eyes. As I stared into his eyes, I became a little boy and innocently stammered that I wanted to achieve *moksha* or liberation. His smile widened and he placed a hand on my head and gave his blessing with, "let it be so!" I was transported to another plane of reality and when I returned to an awareness of my surroundings, he was gone. I marveled at what could still happen in this day and age.

After meditating at the temple, I walked back down and was just in time to meet with a group of pilgrims walking up, surrounding Gurunath.

He called me over and told me that I had missed the morning jalebies (a syrupy sweet beloved in Punjab and surrounding states.) However, he said that the sweet shop was making a new batch and led me back to the shop and we sat down and we had the most delicious jalebies imaginable, as well as a cup of hot chai.

Later in that evening, we went up again. The Naths showed due reverence to Gurunath and allowed us greater access to the Temple then they would normally, and we were able to examine the large number of paintings describing the stories of Babaji's activities more than a thousand years ago. They showed divine personages and great kings paying homage to the Ancient of Days, another epithet for the immortal used by my Gurudev.

Visitors are generally made to sit outside the inner sanctum and observe and listen from afar to the ceremonies inside. We were allowed to sit near the everlasting *dhuni* or fire-pit of Gorakhnath, and had an unparalleled experience of the Arati, a ceremony of light and sound worship offered twice every day. We vibrated with the raw, primeval, indescribable and rhythmic beats of the Nath instruments, which together with the chanting opened the chakras or spinal energy centers of all the participants. These percussion pieces looked like they came from the iron age – they were rough and lethal looking weapons rather than musical instruments.

The highlight came as one of the Naths simply brushed aside the ashes covering the *dhuni*, and the flames leapt up in glory. This *dhuni* was the yogic fire lit by Babaji and has been active for over a thousand years continuously.

We all thirst for such experiences, but we should be warned not to frivolously try to seek out such experiences without the means to modulate the raw energy, which might disrupt our energy centers beyond our capacities to absorb. That is why normal pilgrims are restricted to stay outside the Arti area and can only indirectly hear the ceremony.

The darshan of the flames at the Goddess Temple, on the other hand can be safely experienced as often as grace manifests.

As if the Arati was not enough, we also had the blessing to be allowed into the small cubicle of the *dhibi* itself, a small space just enough to fit three or four of us at a time. There we had the darshan of vision experience of the fire and water, the mystery of the *kundalini shakti*. Of that, we shall speak more of another time!

Although the truly holy places are all within us and it is not necessary to go outwards even to ascend the holy Mount Kailash (the abode of Lord Shiva), it is inspirational and rewarding to go on external pilgrimages, especially so if you can be in the company of a Master.

The Mystery of Gorakhnath

Gorakhnath is the name of a great yogi who was active about one thousand two hundred years ago. His name is known throughout India, sometimes with reverence and awe and sometimes as an object of subtle derision. All great saints in India after that time have been measured by their followings against Him. The followers and devotees of these other yogis and saints generally would make up stories about how their saint somehow defeated Gorakhnath is some form of spiritual duel – this would go on for eight hundred years! Yet such a powerful figure is hardly known in the West. Or is he known but annonymously?

It was during my visit to the massive, but hidden Gorakhnath Temple also called Gorak Dibi at the extinct volcano of Jwala Mukhi, where the legendary immortal Siddha had meditated over a thousand years ago, that I had an opportunity to meet with one of the senior ascetics of the Adi-Nath sampradaya or spiritual lineage.

I stared at the distinctive split ear and large ivory earrings almost hidden by the voluminous hair cascading down the naked shoulders, while listening to an explanation of the indivisibility of Shiva and Shakti. Here was a real Nath yogi, a renowned ascetic belonging to the Gorakhnath monastery in Hardwar. He explained that he was visiting Jwala Mukhi on a training assignment, since it was here where hundreds of young naths are still being trained in the ancient ways, where intense youths in their saffron robes perform the *shramanic* Arti or worship to Gorakhnath.

It has been many years since I had been initiated into the ancient Nath tradition by Yogiraj Gurunath Siddhanath, but the depths and mysteries surrounding them throughout Bharat (India) still astounded me. It is always a delight to meet and listen to a follower of Gorakshanath, who is also known as Gorakhsha or Gorakhnath.

When he started telling me his favorite stories about the exploits of the founder of the lineage, it reminded me that Gorakhnath, although little known now even in the land of his activities, still had a palpable influence throughout the northern parts of India, from the thousands upon thousands of naked *sadhus* who appear during the Kumbha Mela,(the greatest show on earth where 30 million people congregate once every 4 years) to the snake charmers' guild who have kept a thousand year promise to Goraknath that they would release their snakes every year during the naga festival.

Who are the Naths and who is Gorakhnath?

The Naths are the Lords of Yoga. Their tradition goes back to pre-history, and they have also been known as the Siddhas in more recent times. Many of the Siddhas revered in southern India are Naths: Bogarnath, Sundarnath [who became Tirumoolar], Matsyendranath, and Gorakhnath.

As an identifiable group mentioned in historical texts, the Naths became prominent during the early part of the 10th century, with the advent of the Master Yogi, Gorakhnath. He became a renowned miracle worker, to such an extent that he was deified and became known as Shiva-Gorakshanath, or a manifestation of Shiva, and paid the highest possible spiritual tribute of having his own Gayatri mantra, an honor reserved only for the Gods. He was adopted as the Patron deity of Nepal, where to this day, there is a throne for him beside the throne of the King of Nepal, and the fierce tribes of Nepal are called the Gurkhas, in his honor. Thousands of legends sprang up around Gorakhnath throughout the north of Bharat (India), and his temples dominated all of the Punjab by the 15th century, and the Naths had become the main yogic group, with dozens of different sects. However, with the increase in numbers of so-called naths , came the inevitable decrease in the numbers of genuine Naths, and the increasing disrepute brought by fakes extorting money for their magical services. The rise of the Sikhs and the rule of the British Christians brought large-scale persecution of the Naths and the destruction of thousands of Nath temples. Only in recent times has the Nath tradition come back down from the Himalayas and re-established itself quietly. Among the various groups of Naths, many are renunciates, but there has always been a reputable group of house-holders, and that tradition is still very strong, especially in Maharashtra and Rajasthan.

The glory of the Deathless Gorakhnath is less known today than at any other time. He is known as the Nameless One, or as my Master calls Him, the Lightning Standing Still. He is acknowledged as the inventor of the Hatha Yoga system and was the great driving force in popularizing the practice of yoga to the common people by composing the first yogic texts in Hindi, rather than Sanskrit. Many saints, including Kabir, were taught by him or his direct disciples. It is interesting to note that Yoganandaji was born in Gorakpur, which was named after Gorakhnath.

One cold and windy night, as we sat by the night fire amidst the Himalayan mountains, Gurunath my Master related a small parable of Shiva-Goraksha-Babaji. It is an inspiring tale of guidance to aspiring yogis. Once there was a famous yogi who had practiced vigorously for his whole life, and yet had not attained to the final and highest nirvana samadhi. He became filled with rage and decided to end his life. On his way to die, Goraksha was sitting calmly under a tree and asked, "Where are you going, my son?" The frustrated yogi responded, "To die!" and Goraksha calmly responded, "Then die, if you must, but make sure the dying is complete. If you cannot die completely, then come to me and I will teach you to die so perfectly that you will never die again and become deathless." The yogi sat down at Goraksha's feet and in due time attained deathless *niranjana samadhi* under the loving eye of this Guru, Shiva-Gorakshanath.

What fascinates me most about Gorakshanath is that there is a Nath tradition that he is Babaji, or more to the point, that Babaji appeared as Gorakhnath during the 10th to 12th century, and guided the mass of humanity directly during a critical time across the first millenium. The fact of this Reality of Babaji being Shiva-Goraksha was brought to light by my Gurudeva in the year 1967 when he had his life transforming experience of, as he calls Him - the Being about whom nought may be said.[1]

Shiva-Goraksha-Babaji's fame was such and his exploits so awesome that he became the yardstick by which subsequent generations would measure the heights of spirituality. For the following five hundred years, no spiritual Master was complete until his disciples invented a story about a meeting with and the resounding defeat of Gorakhnath !! It appears to be a genetic defect in half-baked disciples that they need to justify their own Guru in some way. From Allum Prabu, to Kabir to Guru Nanak, many a saint had to "defeat" the Master Yogi Gorakhnath as proof of their enlightened state, even though it may be well-known that they were his disciples.

Astoundingly, there are many legends taught about Gorakhnath's exploits that date back to a time more than a thousand years before his activities were historically recorded, that is, before the advent of Christianity. As with the other immortal Siddhas, there are no stories of his ever passing away, and he is said to be residing in the Himalayas and guiding humanity's evolution.

There is one among the many legends concerning his "birth" which I particularly like. It is said that Matsyendranath, who had achieved the deathless immortal state went to Lord Shiva and asked for a disciple who would be greater than he. The blue-throated Lord of Yoga protested that it was not possible - that in all creation, there was none to surpass his state. However, Matsyendranath persisted, and Lord Shiva agreed, and decided that the only way to grant this boon to his favorite devotee was to incarnate a part of Himself, and assumed the spirit of Goraksha, awaiting the moment to manifest. Later, during his travels, Matsyendranath came across a barren woman who asked that she be graced with a child, and in his compassion, he gave her some *vibhuti* or ash from his *dhuni* or yogic fire, and instructed her to eat it.

---

[1]Reference to the documentary film, "Wings to Freedom"

45

At that moment, the spirit of Gorakhsha entered the *vibhuti*, but unfortunately, the woman did not have sufficient faith, and dumped the ash in the cow-dung heap.

Years later, Matsyendranath returned to the woman's village and asked to see the child, and she confessed that she had thrown the ash into the village's mound of cow-dung. Undeterred, Matsendranath asked her to show him the pile, and immediately a lustrous, golden youth appeared, for Goraksha was ready to help the earth and its inhabitants. He teaches us how to cleanse away the dirt that surrounds our souls, the impurities that prevent the inflow and manifestation of our divinity. He is the master of spiritual evolution through the Raja and Hatha yogic practices.

The Rishis, Naths and Siddhas are different names for the immortals, who have reached the pinnacle of evolution and integration. They have dedicated themselves to help the rest of their brothers and sisters. In the ultimate sense, they are one, but they have also chosen to manifest the glory of the Divine in different forms, and it is always tempting to speculate on the relationships between these forms. Babaji has chosen to reveal only a small part of his awesome work, and it would presumptive of us to think we can limit him or his appearances. He had revealed himself in the 1800s to Lahiri Mahasaya, and re-introduced the science of Kriya Yoga to humanity. Whether Gorakhnath is a name that Babaji used at certain times can only be revealed by him, when and if he wishes.

A Call to Battle

Recent world events have forcefully brought home to many of us the realities of both the valor and ugliness of physical and psychological warfare. We are challenged to seek a deeper meaning in these external events and relate them to our values and spiritual path.

We are continuously bombarded by justifications from those who support a war and equally vehement denunciations from those who oppose it. A war is usually justified by the toppling of tyranny and freedom for the helpless oppressed, while the suffering of the innocent and speculations about hidden motives and objectives are used to tarnish those who feel righteous. In fact, most wars are caused by aggression by one party for the sake of land, riches or natural resources.

The experience of humanity from its history is a long series of wars. The sad truth seems to be that warfare has been the result of man's inability to make progress in his evolutionary struggle. Leaders will justify a war, and catalog all the unsuccessful steps taken to reach a peaceful accord – it is always the fault of the other side. Most will be convinced, but some will not accept that everything that could be done was done; after all, who can possibly deny the speculation that there could have been another round of peace talks that might have brought a peaceful resolution! Such is the futility of trying to make sense of the road to war from a purely intellectual perspective – at some point, reason is thrown out, and emotion takes over, and the warrior has to be called in.

At such times, when we are confused, those who follow the yogic path may be inspired to consult the Bhagavad Gita, one of the earliest and most authoritative sources of yogic practice.

The Bhagavad Gita is the instruction by Krishna, an embodiment of the Divine, to Arjuna, a great warrior and king, in the field of battle, between two grand armies, just before they start a war that will destroy most of Northern India and herald the commencement of a dark age.

Arjuna can imagine the horrors which will result from even what he knows to be a just war, and begins to doubt and grow faint-hearted, asking for Divine instruction.

To understand Krishna's response, it would be necessary to briefly review the immediate path that had led to the setting of the Gita. Arjuna and his four brothers were the rightful kings, but due to circumstances, their uncle and cousins had usurped control of the land, and refused to even share any part of it. For thirteen long years, the five brothers and their family had suffered humiliation, assassination attempts, and exile, while their subjects had suffered untold misery, and the injustice of being robbed of their wealth to finance palaces, weapons and armies.

The uncle and cousins had rejected repeated peace proposals. Even Krishna Himself had failed to settle the dispute. Finally, the greedy cousins have rejected letting go of five villages, so that each of the rightful heirs can have at least a parcel of land, and their actions had led to the amassing of these two grand armies, comprising all the great kings and generals in Northern India – two coalitions, one on each side of the dispute.

Arjuna attempted to bring the question of war into a rational framework:

> *We do not know which is the more meritorious for everyone – that we vanquish them or that they vanquish us.*
> Bhagavad Gita 2.6

However, Krishna smiles, as he commences his instruction, for He knows that there can be no rational, moral or ethical basis for war that cannot be disputed. Therefore, He shifts the ground from under Arjuna, by leading him to the spiritual and eternal perspective, that there is no true death or destruction from the battle:

> *That which dwells in every body [the Spirit] is its eternal and indestructible owner. It is not proper therefore for you to lament over any creature.*

48

Bhagavad Gita 2.30
Then Krishna skillfully brings Arjuna back to the practical perspective of his role in life as a warrior and defender of the weak:

> *If you do not fight this righteous battle, you will have failed in your duty, lost your honor and incurred karmic consequences.*
>
> Bhagavad Gita 2.33

Everyone wishes that there were no wars. The Divine Light knows that the cause of all wars is the imperfections and delusions within humanity, and is not easily eradicated. It was the desire and attachment for power and land that had driven their cousins to usurp the kingdom from the rightful heirs. It was anger against those who might have a better claim on the land that had lead to murder attempts, deceits and attempted rape. It was anger that had led to the formation of armies pitting friends and family against each other:

> *When a person even thinks about sensory objects, attachment is developed; attachment gives rise to desire, and desire results in anger.*
>
> Bhagavad Gita 2.62

Since all human actions appear to be 'tainted' by delusions, one might be tempted to counsel non-action, but not Krishna, who warns that non-action is not a solution, when action is called for:

> *A person does not attain release from action by not acting, nor does she attain perfection by mere renunciation of action.*
>
> Bhagavad Gita 3.4

After all, sometimes when you refrain from doing something tha tyou should, there can be negative consequences. What happens when someone is lying injured and passers-by ignore the person and do not give help? The person dies and non-action is the cause. There is a way out, a way to overcome the vicious cycle of war – it is to overcome the delusions caused by desires and attachments:

> *A person whose heart is unperturbed in the midst of calamities and free from desires in the midst of pleasures, from whom attachment, fear and rage have departed, is called a wise-one with steady reason.*
>
> Bhagavad.Gita 2.56

In the previous example, it is the fear of getting involved or possible harm to oneself that causes the non-action.

Krishna advocates that only the yogic path of self-realization can free a person from the *karmic* consequences of action:

> *Action cannot bind the person who has cast off all action through yoga, whose doubts have been destroyed by knowledge and who has realized his Self.*
>
> Bhagavad.Gita. 3.41

Accordingly, the ideal man of action, the ideal man of peace is without ego, a yogi who has achieved Self-Realization:

> *The person who acts after giving up all desire, who is free from any sort of 'mine-ness' or egoism – that person alone attains tranquility.*
>
> Bhagavad.Gita. 2.71

The message is clear, whether we are ready to accept it or not – war is caused by the ignorance and imperfect understanding of humanity, and cannot be resolved by rational, moral and ethical means. Only when all of mankind has attained to higher states of consciousness, will war cease.

The external war is a reflection of the internal war within all of us. It is the highest good for a person to practice yoga in the hope of achieving

Self-Realization. For in this way, the root of violence and war is eradicated in that person. There is a ripple effect by which one yogi will affect others around to attain equanimity and liberation from the cycle of birth and death.

From a yogic perspective, each one of us needs to focus on how to eradicate the causes of war within us. An external war is the clarion call for all of us to intensify our practice to transform ourselves and achieve Self-Realization.

Jesus the Siddha

I have often wondered what Jesus was like - what he actually said and did two thousand years ago. It is sad that what we have in the gospels of the New Testament are sketchy accounts made one or more generations after he left. Many more gospels were destroyed by the Orthodox Church authorities and the four left were then edited, and revised by overzealous scribes. However, here and there the presence of such a mighty figure still shines through.

It is interesting to speculate that Jesus, during his so-called missing years, might have gone to India and learned from the wise sages of the time. There were great yogis belonging to the Nath tradition, often also called Siddhas in later times, who had established great centers of learning in those days. They cared neither to be called Vedic Rishis or Buddhist Bodhisattvas – their compassion knew no such artificial boundaries, for Yoga is not a religion. They sought to teach union with the Divine, the Nameless One.

The chronicles of the Naths have recorded that a great soul from the land of the Hebrews visited them during the time of King Shalivahan and Emperor Kanishka (around the time of Jesus) and was initiated into their tradition. He was given the name Ishanath. It would be easy to dismiss such a record if not for the fact that throughout the land of Kashmir in the North of India are other records of this enigmatic prophet and holy man.

The Siddhas are those who have achieved perfection. Their goal is to perfect themselves while still in the material body – to bring divinity into matter, to transmute matter into spirit. This was, is, and will always be the Alchemy of Total Transformation. Another mark of the Siddhas is their miraculous powers including bringing the dead back to life. There are many stories of their powers in the tales of the Naths. In recent times, Yogananda has recounted in the Autobiography of a Yogi, how Babaji brought back to life, a disciple who had jumped to his death to demonstrate his faith in the Ancient of Days. Many of the Siddhas transformed their bodies such that they would not decay and therefore virtually immortal. Since the Siddhas had mastered and transformed materiality, they no longer have any attachments or attractions for wealth or power.

Was Jesus a yogi and a Siddha? In Matthew 5:48, he says: "Be ye therefore perfect, even as your Father which is in heaven is perfect."

Jesus is asking his disciples to do some work, not just to believe in something. He is not asking them to wish they were perfect or even try to be better people. The goal is to be as perfect as the Divine. Hardly, the goal preached in sermons nowadays.

Again, when a rich young man came to the Master and expressed his desire to become a disciple, Jesus responded to him:

> *If you wish to be perfect, go and sell all you have, and give to the poor and so that you will have treasure in heaven; then come and follow me.*
> Matthew 19:21

Here, Jesus is giving a recipe for perfection -- it is to give up attachment to material things. He is often misinterpreted as preaching that wealth is an impediment to spirituality, but that only reflects the lack of understanding of the underlying priniciples. The key is that he is not asking the young man to just give some or even most of his wealth, but to give all - this is only possible from the sense of detachment. It doesn't matter if you only have one penny, if you are attached to it, then you will not attain to perfection.

Jesus performed many miracles during his time of teaching including bringing back to life the dead Lazurus. The common factor in all of the gospels is the miracles and healing powers. Jesus consistently and continuously demonstrated the *siddhis* or powers of a Siddha.

In the teachings of the Naths / Siddhas there are techniques used to open the spiritual eye (the third-eye or sixth energy center of the subtle body.) The Light of the Divine is seen when the third eye is opened, and consequently, the body is transformed and filled with this Light. Listen to the words of the Master:

> *The light of the body is the eye; if, therefore, your eye be single, your whole body shall be full of light.*
> Matthew 6:22

The practices that Jesus brought back to his homeland from India are not easy to find in the gospels anymore. However, here and there, we can discover some hints.

The Siddhas taught silence as a way to commune with the Divine within. Listen to St. Paul in 1 Cor. 6:10: "Let him keep silence in the Church; and let him speak to himself and to God."

The Siddhas advocated fasting to control one's desires and it is recorded that Jesus went into the desert after his anointing by John the Baptist and fasted for forty days. He went deep into his meditations and overcame his ego. This is illustrated by the story of his temptation by the devil in Matthew 4:3-7:

> *And when the tempter came to him, he said, "If you are the Son of God, command that these stones be made bread. But he answered and said, "It is written, Man shall not live by bread alone, but by every word that comes out of the mouth of God. Then the devil took him up into the holy city and set him on a pinnacle of the temple and said to him, "If you are the Son of God, cast yourself down; for it is written that He shall give his angels charge concerning you; and in their hands they shall bear you up, lest at any time you hurt your foot against a stone." Jesus said to him, "It is written again, you shall not tempt the Lord thy God."*

Jesus achieved Self-Realization by rejecting the ego tempter. He also rejected the use of his powers for sake of satisfying his ego.

The *kundalini* energy is dormant in all beings until activated by the Siddha practices - it is usually depicted as a serpent. This serpent *kundalini* is latent in the first energy center or *chakra* at the base of the spine, and has to be raised up to the seventh *chakra* for liberation from the ego - Self-Realization. Compare the following:

> *And as Moses lifted up the serpent in the wilderness, even so must the son of Man be lifted up.*
> John 3:14

More mysterious to the uninitiated are his words talking about have a secret stash of meat! In John 4:32, Jesus says:

> *I have meat to eat that you know not of.*

However, in the writings of the Siddhas, the tongue is called meat and there are practices by which the tongue is used to obtain the nectar of immortality which satisfies all hunger and thirst. Through these practices, the Siddha can stop all vital signs and be as the dead to others. Whenever they wish, they can revive themselves. Such is the power of these yogis.

The Siddhas taught the unity of all beings and taught meditations in which they visualized their worst enemy and removed their hate and anger, replacing negative emotions with pure love for all. Listen to Jesus:

> *But I say to you, Love your enemies, bless them that curse you, do good to them that hate you, and pray for them which despitefully use you and persecute you.*
> Matthew 5:44

Truly, Jesus was a Master and Siddha.

Parables

The Master Jesus used parables in his teachings. I have always found parables to be the best means to communicate key spiritual concepts. Parables have a great impact and are remembered long after philosophical discussions have been forgotten. They have been used by the yogis for thousands of years.

In my workshops and seminars, I always use stories and parables as illustrations of certain principles that are important on the path of Self-Realization.

The following two parables are among my favorite. I had written them down many years ago and do not know their source or who translated them. Over the years, I have updated them by eliminating some unnecessary parts and adding my own comments and explanations. But my sincere thanks goes to those who strive to communicate ancient knowledge and wisdom.

Parable 1: Preparing for Life

Once upon a time, there was a great city in India, along the banks of the holy river Ganges. Its people followed a peculiar political philosophy, according to which any of its citizens could become its ruler just for the asking. However, there was a term-limit of five years. After the fifth year, the king would be bound hand and foot, ferried across the river Ganges to the other bank and thrown as prey to the wild and hungry beasts infesting the forest on that side.

Naturally, very few chose to become the king. Only those who desperately wanted to enjoy themselves for at least five years and did not really care what happened after that time would take the job. However, when their term ended, many a king wished he had not chosen this self-ordained termination - for mercilessly and speedily he was dispatched by the ministers to the other bank of the river to face his doom. Not a single king, despite all his tears and pleadings and bribery, had escaped this doom.

It was the custom of the throng of people to gather like vultures on the bank of the river Ganges every fifth year to see the king making his unceremonious exit. On such occasions, invariably they heard the piteous entreaties of the king for a lease of life which, as was usual, fell on deaf ears.

This time however, the people were rather sorry because the incumbent king was a righteous ruler and instead of spending all his time on wine, women and song, he had put the welfare of his people in the forefront and was the best king in their long history. But the law was the law, and he would need to be sent to the other shore.

They were surprised to see the king coming to the wharf maintaining his regal dignity and smiling at everyone. The king was followed by his retinue of ministers. The boat was there ready for the king to embark. Looking at the ministers the king said, "Well, aren't I still your king until I reach the other bank of the river?" They, in unison, said, "Yes, your majesty". The king said, "In that case I feel I have not been honored properly. This boat is not rigged properly. It is unbecoming of a King to sit on the hard plank of the boat. So get me cushions and pillows and arrange them in such a way that I can have a comfortable trip to the other bank of the Ganges." The ministers carried out the king's command immediately. The king's seat was made comfortable. The king smiled at them and in a waved cheerful to them, as he sailed out to the other side.

The old ferryman, who was in charge of the boat was surprised to see the king in such good humor. He thought that the king perhaps was unaware of his doom. Ferrying the boat slowly, eyeing the king out of the corner of his eye, he asked the king how he could keep himself cool and collected despite the fact that he would soon be a feast for wild beasts.

On hearing this, the king laughed loudly and burst into a song of joy. The ferryman was all the more perplexed. He mused for a while and said to the king, "If your Majesty is thinking of escaping from me. I have to say humbly but firmly that I will at all costs stop you. I have to take all precautions - so please permit me to bind you to your seat." The king laughed again, but permitted himself to be bound to the seat.

The boat had sailed half way when the ferryman asked the king whether he was not afraid of the wild beasts on the other bank of the river. The king in surprise uttered, "What did you say? Wild beasts! Where? On the other side of the Ganges? No. You obviously don't know what has happened. I shall tell you what I did. Listen. You have not been to the other bank of the river for the past five years nor have you noticed the trafficking that has been going on all these five years on the waters of this mighty river. There is no wild forest on the other side of this river, and there are no wild beasts either. I was not like the other kings when I was ruling the country. Right from the moment I assumed kingship, the thought that I would be unceremoniously and mercilessly sent to my doom after my term was completed haunted me. I felt I should find a way out. Though at first this haunting thought of my doom disturbed me no end and could have prevented me from enjoying the comforts of kingship, I mastered my fears and desires and I drew up a five year plan. I could of course not avert going to the other bank of the Ganges after the fifth year. But I felt I had the power in me to make a heaven of hell." The king stopped momentarily and asked for a cup of water.

He then continued, "I decided to make the forest on the other bank of the Ganges, which till now was a hell to all the other rulers, a heaven for me. So during the first year of my rule I sent a group of hunters and ordered them to kill all the wild animals in the forest on the other bank of the river. In the second year, I sent two thousand woodcutters to fell the trees and clear the forest. In the third year, I sent masons, architects and engineers to the same place and ordered them to build lovely palaces, develop graceful pleasure gardens, beautiful parks, swimming pools and lovely stadiums for me, and so I made it a paradise. In the fourth year, I selected trustworthy and loyal men from my court, appointed them as ministers, ordered them to go to my paradise and plan how a country could be made beautiful and righteously ruled. In the fifth year, picking and choosing those of the people who were good, virtuous and loyal to me, I told them of my plan and they agreed to migrate to my new kingdom. So, now I'm really going to my true home to assume kingship. Oh! Ferryman, look for yourself how grand my city is, for we are nearing it now. Just glance that way. Don't you see my ministers in their best, with garlands in their hands, ready to welcome me? Don't you see the musicians and singers with their welcoming songs and melodies. I have mastered my fate. Am I not a Man of Destiny? If you want, you too can come and be my ferryman."

The ferryman did indeed see on the other bank of the river a mighty city of splendor and glory. He saw also the colorful gathering awaiting their king. An elephant all-decked out was waiting, ready to receive the king!

The life that we lead in this world is as the life of the king of a fixed term. We are the self-appointed rulers of our lives, but death awaits all of us, waiting in the wings to take us to the wild beasts. We cannot bargain for even a second of life beyond our allotment. We lay waste our precious powers, thoughtlessly vegetating in front of our television sets, earning, spending, and indulging our senses. Then when the sad end comes, we blame our fate, our stars, or even our gods, not realizing that it is all of our own making.

But instead of wasting our time on earth, if we followed the wise king's example, we can strive with foresight, determination, discrimination and steadfastness to plan out for ourselves a path of happiness. We can transition to a glorious era of eternal peace and unalloyed bliss by facing the challenges of the interaction of our forces in a world limited by space, time and causation.

This inherent power in us to overcome our fate is called dharma. Fate is undoubtedly the result of our own wrong actions, our karma. By using this inherent power in us, we can lift ourselves to such heights where the effect of the forces of fate will not be felt by us. This in short is what the parable tells us – follow dharma to overcome karma. The highest dharma is the path of Self-Realization. Instead of indulging our senses in pursuit of pleasure in the world, we can use our energy to achieve liberation and enlightenment from the cycle of suffering.

Parable 2: The Carnival of Life

In an ancient land, there ruled a king of the Solar dynasty. He was noted for his wisdom, thoughtfulness and courage. Although a great warrior, he was righteous and peace-loving. During his benevolent rule, the country became prosperous as well as the creative leader in arts, literature, music, commerce and philosophy. There was peace in the land as never before.

To ensure the spiritual welfare of his people, he built as many temples as there were deities worshipped by them. The splendor of his achievements was unparalleled. The people were contented.

As time passed, the king became old, but had no heir to follow him. This worried his ministers considerably, but they did not know how to approach the subject. In time, the king became more and more inward-looking and spent his time on spiritual pursuits. It became apparent to his ministers that he was preparing to transition into the next life. They became desperate and gathered the courage to approach their sovereign.

After paying their respects, the chief minister came forward with folded hands and said, "Majesty, we are greatly distressed and would ask you to solve a dire problem facing our land."

The king was puzzled, "I am not aware of any serious problem facing our people. What can it be? Tell me and it shall be removed so that you can be at ease once again!"

The wise minister nodded his head and responded, "Lord, your people are happy, contented and have no material or spiritual wants, thanks to your righteous rule. But if you should leave us for the other world, who can we rely on to rule us so ably and efficiently, so justly and judiciously, so lovingly and thoughtfully? Our country has not been blessed with an heir to succeed your Highness. This is the cause of our anxiety."

The king smiled and said, "My beloved ministers, thank you for bringing this concern to me. I will soon choose my heir, to ensure a smooth transition. My heir will be a just and wise ruler with great discrimination and single-minded in his love for the people." This reply surprised the ministers for they knew it was no easy task to choose a worthy heir for their unparalleled king, but they had faith in his judgment and waited for the drama to unfold.

The king soon gave his ministers detailed instructions for the organization and building of a huge carnival, the size of a town. He architected the layout, types of attractions to be displayed, and the games to be played. He then asked his ministers to go and announce to the people that he was giving them a chance to show their determination and discrimination. Somewhere in the carnival, in the center of attraction, was a place he had chosen to stay in. The person who recognized him and identified him in the carnival would be chosen as his heir.

The wise king had designed the stalls and booths to be very tempting and distracting for the people, so that only the strong-willed, persevering and discriminating individual would be capable of identifying him, in the middle of so many attractions.

On entering the carnival, people became mesmerized by the number and variety of stalls, booths and performances. There were lotteries, shooting galleries, burlesque shows, comedy and magic shows, swimming pools, performing animals, arts and crafts galore from all over the world, tasty food stalls satisfying the palate of one and all, and many other items of display. The carnival ground was resplendent in displays of banners, flags and streamers. The place provided fun, frolic and mirth not only to the young but also to the old. There was even a temple built in one corner, with a large tank filled with crystal clear water. No one who entered wished to leave this carnival.

The carnival was opened day and night and never closed, and would operate until the heir was chosen. Tens of thousands of people from all over the country came to see the magnificent carnival. The stalls were alluring, the booths enticing, the dancing halls tempting and the theatres enthralling. Caught up in such attractions, people forgot that they had gone there to identify the king and thereby become the heir. Some who had a degree of patience, tried to see if they could identify the king in any of the people stationed in the stalls. So strenuous was this task that in the end they gave it up and took to enjoying the objects displayed instead.

Many days passed and then came a young knight riding a horse from a neighboring town. He decided not to waste his time by walking and so rode on horseback into the carnival with the single aim of finding the king.

With his subtle mind he examined the sights that he saw and applied his discriminative faculty to separate the revelers and performers. Although his mind was yoked to the goal of identifying the king, he did not despise the sights that he saw nor the sweet melodies that he heard. Outwardly he seemed to enjoy everything that came his way with a smile and a nod of his head, but his keen and incisive intellect was trying to separate the illusive carnival play from the reality of royalty.

After some time, even he seemed to lose heart, for in vain had he searched in all the likely places. However, in his innermost heart of hearts, the yearning for the goal sustained him, releasing an extra spurt of energy overcoming his disappointment. Finally, he came to the temple, the only place he had not yet searched. To purify himself, he had a bath in the temple-tank, and with reverence entered the temple, going straight to the holy of holies, the inner sanctum. There he had a vision of the deity of his heart, but not the presence of the king.

The young man than applied his contemplative discrimination. It felt right that the king would be found in the temple, but the knight failed to find any trace of him, even after going around the temple three times. His mind became quiescent and he stood apart and in a flash had a vision of the king seated in a room behind a secret passage. Immediately, he examined the walls of the inner sanctum and saw a carved block of stone which projected slightly more than rest. He had to use all of his strength to pull on it, but slowly it came out. Behind the stone, the resolute young man saw a secret passage.

It was dark, but he stepped into the darkness feeling his way with his hands. Soon he came to another stone-structure, with a projecting square block. Lifting it, he slid it down the wall. A blinding white light streamed out from a beautifully decorated chamber. The smiling king was seated on a golden throne in the centre of the carpeted floor and jeweled ceiling.

After his long search, the young knight was speechless at the magnificence of the Lord of his land. He prostrated himself before the king paying his respects. The king too felt happy, for the Divine Maker had ushered into his presence a worthy heir.

This world with its myriad attractions and distractions is the Carnival of Life. The Divine Creator is the ruler. He has sent us into the world not only to enjoy its beauties but also to recognize that we soon lose our identification with the Supreme, when immersed in the attractions of the world of objects, emotions and thoughts.

We can only realize our True Self if we act like the young knight and apply our discriminative faculties with perseverance, to unravel the real from the unreal. We should not allow the objects of the senses to entice us away from our unity with the Divine, but at the same time we need not despise the world of objects. It is possible to enjoy everything that comes our way, and yet not become slaves of enjoyment. This requires the constant and continuous application of self-discipline.

Part 2

Pathways to the Light

84,000 Paths!

What is Yoga?
State of Self-Realization
Pathway to Self-Realization
Process of Self-Realization
Union with the Divine
Shiva-Shakti
Soul-jiva to spirit-Atman
Super-consciousness: Samadhi
Divine Consciousness: Samadhi
Cosmic Consciousness: Samadhi
Liberation: Moksha
Freedom from Rebirth: Moksha
Freedom from Karma: Moksha
Enlightenment
Spiritual Evolution

Why are there so many different yogas?
As many as there are types of people
Everyone in every life has a chance
to find the Divine Within
A yoga to suit each and every soul
No soul left behind, no soul forgotten.
Kriya Yoga
Hatha Yoga and Raja Yoga
Jnana Yoga
Tantra Mantra and Yantra
Kundalini Yoga
Bhakti Yoga and Karma Yoga
This life is precious
Death is inevitable
Departure time is unknown
Why waste energy on passing bhoga?
Start now the practice of yoga.

Yoga is not a religion. It is the science of Self-Realization. One does not have to belief in the Divine to practice yoga – one does have to belief that there is something more to us than we are aware of at the moment. We have to belief that we are not utilizing all our capabilities nor have we reached our highest potential.

A confusion arises when yoga is enmeshed with the Hindu religion in the minds of spiritual aspirants. This is unavoidable as the development of the science of yoga took place over many thousands of years continuously in India. It is steeped in the culture and language of the Indian sages. The spiritual aspirant has to see through the externals and grasp the essentials to resonate with the Divine within. Then all confusion vanishes.

It must also be kept in mind that yoga is an experiential system and must be practiced. No amount of book reading will enable one to realize the words of the *yogis*. The personal practice of a spiritual aspirant per instructions from a qualified guide is called *sadhana*, and the aspirant becomes a practitioner or *sadak*.

The practices of yoga are based on belief in the existence of hidden potentialities in man. This is not to be taken on faith alone, but by verification, initially through a Master, and then through one's own practice.

Over the ages, different types of Yogas have been developed to suit the temperaments of different truth seekers. As systems developed, many varieties of each system also came into being due to the different levels of realization by the practitioners. Also, over time, systems became unappreciated or lost and others changed names or became merged with the leading practices of the day. There is continuous movement in the systems of yoga due to changes in the consciousness of the masses and the appearances of some particular towering sage or another.

Types of Yogic Discipline

Kriya Yoga is the quintessential yogic practice. This was taught by Babaji in the primordial times to the Sun (Surya), who then taught it to Manu (the first man). It had been handed down through the solar dynasty of Ramachandra, but was lost to the masses during the dark ages, until Babaji again introduced it by initiating Lahiri Mahasaya in the 19th century.

Some aspects of Kriya Yoga were divided into Hatha and Raja Yoga during the dark age so that the masses could have a practice that would help them with the spiritual evolution. Hatha Yoga comprises the first four steps of the Eight-fold path called Ashtanga Yoga: *yama, niyama, asana, pranayama* – it is the preparation for Raja Yoga which comprises of: *pratyahara, dharana, dhyana* and *samadhi*. Instead of trying to explain all these now steps now, they will be individually dealt with in later sections.

Hatha Yoga has been misidentified as a series of gymnastics and the dreams of contortionists. In actuality it is a process leading to the union of Ha and Tha , the sun and the moon, Shiva and Shakti, through the arousal of the dormant *kundalini* energy. This *kundalini* or the primordial cosmic energy in motion within the microcosm of our bodies is awakened through the discipline of the physical body, purification of the *nadis*, or subtle energy channels, and controlling the Life Force called *prana*. The mind is united to *prana*, and by conscious breathing techniques called *pranayama*, mind is controlled. The nervous system and its subtle counterpart - the related *nadis* and *chakras* or the "concentrated wheels of energy transformers" are purified and *kundalini* awakened. When the *kundalini* rises from the first energy center at the perineum to the seventh in the crown, then Self-Realization happens. Properly speaking, it is the Divine Mother or active aspect of Shiva that resides in the body of men and women in the form of *kundalini*. The Hatha yogi relies on *asana* and *pranayama* to raise the *kundalini*. There are additional methods employed such as *Japa* (repetition of the *mantras*) of the names of the Divine Mother, prayers, rituals and visualizations to achieve the awakening and Her eventual union with Sadashiva, the Lord in the *sahasrara* or seventh *chakra*. There are many schools of Tantra, but it appears that only Samaya Tantra has proven capable under the guidance of a Master of leading to *moksha* or Liberation.

The misunderstanding and misuse of Tantric Saktism by unqualified people has lead to the incorporation of sex and drugs into so-called Tantric rituals. These can be hindrances on the path. Everything in this world can be abused for base purposes, even if it is something as profound as Yoga.

To those who seek liberation through direct knowledge has been given the Jnana Yoga practice. This is a difficult path during this time of still rather low mass consciousness. The process is one of discrimination, intellectualization and detachment, exercising and stilling the mind, achieving the "Liberation through direct realization of the Truth." The human body generally is not utilized in this yoga – it is considered a hindrance or an illusion at best.

The two favored paths for the helping the majority of people along their spiritual evolution are Karma Yoga and Bhakti Yoga.

Karma Yoga practice is for those who need to perform activities, rather than sitting for meditation. However, it is important for all yogis of all paths. It is based on the premise that since every action performed by a person gives rise to a reaction to that person, the only way to effectively remove oneself from this cycle is to offer all actions to the Divine. Practically, it means to perform actions without taking credit for them, and in turn, not taking the negative consequences. This is an on-going process which eventually results in a person totally dedicated as an instrument of the Divine Will.

For those who seek the Divine through devotion, has been given Bhakti Yoga. This is well-known to everyone and is the most visible form of religious worship. Besides the outward use of chanting and ceremonies, in the yogic tradition of *bkakti* is also the use of *mantras* or formulae of power for purifying the mind and tuning in to certain aspects of the Divine. This is the yoga of love and devotion, with self-surrender and dedication of all the disciple's resources to attain the ultimate reality. Study of the scriptures, constant *japa*, non-attachment while doing one's duties and always remembering the Lord with self-surrender are the keys of this Yoga. This is a Yoga beginning with dualism – the Lord and the devotee. First, one attains to the state of "I am thine", then to "Thou art mine", and ultimately to "I and my Father are One"

From ancient times, the transmission of spiritual *sadhana* or discipline has been from Guru to disciple, and the type of process or yoga given would be confidential and specific to the disciple's needs. There could not be different types of yoga to be trademarked, since each disciple's yoga could be different, and the only broad categorization would be by the name of the Guru.

In recent times, since the middle ages, there has been an attempt to distinguish different aspects of Yoga, and put some aspects on a higher plane to others. This has resulted in a proliferation of "yogas," some of which are incomplete.

Evolutionary and non-evolutionary paths

It is the goal of Kriya Yoga to achieve the Union of Shiva and Shakti, to realize our true Being. This will be achieved by many souls in the course of an evolutionary cycle, and by only a few during a devolutionary cycle. Physical Evolution in humanity has been shown by science to be in the spine (together with the brain) and in order for the achievement of this goal of Union, a true spiritually evolutionary Yoga must focus on the subtle spine with specific techniques.

There are so-called systems which do not provide for evolution through the spine, but may provide for mental or psychological or emotional healing and peace. They should be identified as non-evolutionary. Every seeker must identify their goal and chose the appropriate vehicle for achieving their goal. However, it must be pointed out that on the broad level, any positive activity can be classified as evolutionary if it helps in some way to integrate the spiritual and material worlds within us. Even if someone were to abstain from any type of yoga as well as harmful actions, that person would still, after a million years of births and deaths, have attained to higher states of consciousness. This is not what we are discussing. We are here to look at faster methods of catapulting the consciousness to attain a million years of normal evolution within a single lifetime!

Natha

When I talk to people, there are always questions about Kriya Yoga, and then more and more have become curious about the Naths as well. Who are these mysterious beings?

Natha means Master or Lord and in the highest sense is properly applied to the Lord Shiva Himself.

The concept of lineage or *paraparam* is of paramount importance within the many different sects of Naths. However, they all trace their origins to the lord of yoga, Lord Shiva Himself. From Lord Shiva or the Adinath has emanated various aspects to form the Celestial hierarchy of the Nine Naths, responsible for Cosmic Evolution.

In turn, the Nine Celestial Naths have manifested on Earth in various forms to guide humanity for whole world cycles. Such a one is Gorakshanath, who has been guiding earth's evolution for sixteen and half million years.

In a more mundane sense, Natha is also the name of an ancient Himalayan tradition of practical yogic mysticism founded by Shiva-Goraksha-Babaji. The Masters of this tradition are also called Nathas. There have been many great beings who have tread the earth bearing the title of Natha. Through their practice of siddha yoga they have attained tremendous powers, *siddhis*, and are sometimes referred to as *siddha yogis* (accomplished or fully enlightened ones.)

The words of such beings naturally penetrate deeply into the consciousness of their devotees, causing mystical awakenings. The *darshan* or vision of a Natha is life-changing and eagerly sought by all the spiritual aspirants since ancient times.

Long before the Buddha, Nathas have always refused to recognize caste distinctions in spiritual pursuits. Their Satgurus initiate from the highest to the lowest, according to spiritual worthiness, not according to wealth, power, or caste.

The continuous stream or tradition of yogic transmission is called the Natha Sampradaya. Unfortunately, the highest knowledge of the Naths has been discarded during the last five hundred years of the dark age and they were persecuted by new religious fanatics as well as by foreign rulers. Now, the Nathas are only remembered as the source of Hatha (including Kundalini) as well as Raja Yoga. From 900 CE to 1500 CE, the Natha Siddhas were also responsible for establishing various alchemical and *tantric* lineages. In fact, all yogic lineages can be traced back to some Natha or other, just as all Yoga flows ultimately from Lord Shiva.

The Goal

Besides the disregard for the rigid caste system, the Naths also differed from the later yogic schools in that they attained to the transformation of the physical body into an immutable immortal body. The goal of the Nath Siddha is not only *moksha*, that is release from conditioned existence, it is to be a Jivanmukti – liberation in the body or physical immortality. The Siddha transcends the laws of nature, breaking out of the bonds of human existence. He is not bound by Death or by Karma. There is a transmutation of the material into the Divine. Theirs was the alchemy of total transformation.

Guru-Disciple Relationship

Another distinctive trait of the Naths was the focus on the relationship between the Master and disciple. Many legends have been retained to illustrate the importance of faith, grace, and mystical powers in the tradition. This is especially true in the case of the two most glorious of the Naths – Matsyendranath and Gorakshanath.

Once upon a time, Lord Shiva appeared in the bottom of the ocean to instruct the Goddess Parvati in the highest aspects of Yoga. It so happened that a young *yogi* had been swallowed by a huge fish while meditating on the sea-shore. The fish swam near to where Lord Shiva and Parvati were at the bottom of the sea, and so it happened that the *yogi* heard everything that the Lord was saying. When Lord Shiva (Adinatha) had finished, He asked if the Goddess had understood, and the *yogi* also answered from the belly of the whale.

From then onwards, the young *yogi* now known as Matsyendranatha, became the foremost and excellent disciple of Shiva. He then prayed to the Lord to send him a disciple who would be a greater *yogi* then himself. The only way for Shiva to fulfill this wish was to manifest Himself and He appeared as Gorakhnatha, to become Matsyendrantha's disciple. They played this Divine drama to help all sincere spiritual aspirants.

There are many stories and legends concerning the Guru-disciple relationship of Matsyendranath and Gorakhnath. One such story illustrates the disciple's desire to see the Guru, as well as his reverence for the Master.

It is said that once when Guru and disciple had gone on separate journeys, Matsyendranath went into deep seclusion and was hidden from Gorakhnath. Wishing to see his Guru, Gorakhnath searched far and wide and came to the kingdom of Nepal, where the people did not receive him with sufficient respect. He saw that they had very bad collective *karma* and resolved to help them to work through their negativity. In the mystical plane, there are beings called *nagas*, symbolically represented as wise serpents and snakes that were responsible for the rain. He caught them by his powers and sat on them and hence became known as Nagaraja – King of Nagas. On the material plane, He took the clouds, fastened them in one of his bundles, sat on them, and remained motionless in deep meditation for twelve years. During that time, no rain fell in Nepal, and the people grew desperate.

74

The king of Nepal asked his wise counselors for a solution, but everything they tried, from threats, soldiers, food, money, and pretty girls all failed to move the Mahayogi. Finally, one of his advisors suggested that they should ask Matsyendranath, the Guru of Gorakhshanath for help.

The king sent out messengers to every corner of India to look for the great Master. Eventually, one came back with the report of his whereabouts. The king immediately travelled to a far-off mountain to seek the help of Matsyendranath, and after much adventure and hardship persuaded him to come to Nepal. As His Master approached, Gorakhnath, out of respect for His Guru, immediately rose up from his seat, and the *nagas* were released. The heavens poured down with rain. That was how the people of Nepal were saved by the reverence of a disciple for His Master.

To this day, Gorakhnath is the patron God of Nepal.

Wahe Guru

Shiva-Gorakhsha-Babaji
Gorakhshanatha
Gorakhnatha
Goraksha
Gorakh

Unborn
Undying
Lightning standing still
Eternal Youth of sixteen summers

Eternal Now
Ancient of Days
Nameless One
The Great Sacrifice
Babaji

The Light that lights the Light within us
Sanatana
Sat Nam Shri Wahe Guru

The Power of Kundalini

The word *kundalini* can be derived from the word kundala which means "coil" and refers to the symbol of the coiled serpent. Just like a coiled spring, it possesses potential energy ready to be awakened as the spring is unleashed. It is a nuclear power station within each of us, ready to be turned on. However, this might never happen during a life-time. The presence of *kundalini* indicates that we are only utilizing a small proportion of our potential - like the oft-repeated but not well-understood truism that we are only using a tenth of our mind.

The word *kundalini* can also be derived from the root *kund* which means "pit" and refers to the place where the kundalini resides – that is between the first and second chakras in the subtle body, where it lies dormant.

Kundalini is the spark of the cosmic Shakti, the Divine Mother or divine Creative Matrix (Goddessence) that is present as potential divinity in each human being. When it is awakened, it opens all the energy centers on its path to the crown center, where it unites with the divine consciousness, gracing one with the state of God-Realization.

This individuated divine power is also described as "serpent power" because it is often visualized as a small red snake coiled three and half times around a *shivalinga*, the symbol of divine consciousness, and of the universe itself.

There is a fine energy channel running in the center of the subtle spine, overlaying the physical spine. This central energy channel called *sushumna nadi* runs from the first energy center at the perineum up to the seventh center in the crown. It is closed at the bottom by the head of the serpent *kundalini* and so is dormant.

The goal of yogic techniques is to awaken the sleeping serpent so that the opening to the *sushumna* is unblocked. When refined life-force energy flows up the central channel, each energy center in turn "lights up" until the seventh is attained. This is the process of Self-Realization.

The *kundalini*, being an aspect of the Goddessence is both the cause of keeping us in the limited consciousness of ignorance, as well as the liberator from the suffering of life and deliverer into the freedom of super-conscious states. This corresponds with the concept of Maya which both the power that keeps us enthralled in the illusive nature of relativity and also the power that releases the sincere practitioner into realization of the absolute consciousness of reality.

The symbology of the three coils has many layers of meaning and can be understood to refer to:

- The three *gunas* or principles governing material manifestation; these are the principles of light, motion and inertia.
- The three *shaktis* of will (*ichchha*), action (*kriya*) and knowledge (*jnana*) which are necessary for the formation of name, form and ideation
- The manifestation of Creative Shakti as:
  o Nada – primordial sound or vibration
  o Bindu – the primordial source or point of manifestation
  o Bija – the seed or medium of creation

In some yogic texts, *kundalini* is said to have eight coils, symbolizing the eight *chakras* and the eight powers or *siddhis* of perfections, which arise from the awakening of *kundalini*.

During the process of physical manifestation, the *kundalini* moves down from the seventh chakra to the first inside the *sushumna nadi* and as it rests around the *shivalinga*, it closes the central channel, obstructing the path to divinity. This is the downward path from spirit to matter.

78

Only through the sincere practice of Yoga can the sleeping *kundalini* be awakened and Self-Realization attained. This is the return journey home – the process of spiritual evolution, back to the Source of All. There is a contemporary misunderstanding that the arousal of *kundalini* can be dangerous. The term *kundalini* psychosis has even been coined to describe the various conditions that are alleged to be caused by misdirected *kundalini*. It must be made clear that *kundalini* is intelligent and will not take a wrong route. It will only rise when the conditions are correct and the central channel is purified. So what is really going on?

These distracting and sometimes debilitating conditions are caused by excessive *prana* (life-force energy in the breath and in our food) or misdirected *prana*. When people with damaged energy channels try to practice the powerful spiritual disciplines which require control of life-force energy, there can be negative consequences. Even when such people come near *yogis* or high energy spots, there can be *prana* overload. Some people are born with damaged nervous systems or damage their nervous systems by drug usage or even accidents. Damaged nervous systems simultaneously lead to damaged energy systems in the subtle body. It is necessary to repair the damage prior to spiritual practice.

The primary systems of yogic discipline that enable the rising of Kundalini Shakti and her union at the seventh *chakra* with Divine Consciousness are scientific processes which need experienced guides and should not be learned through books or those who are not qualified to lead practitioners on the path.

What You Need To Do Yoga

There are many shops and businesses catering to pursuits in sports or hobbies. If one should take up golfing, there are bewildering numbers of golf clubs called irons, woods, drivers and such, as well as shoes and clothing that one would need to purchase. In the same manner, there is growing market in supplying the needs of the "Yoga" community. Yoga mats, stylish clothing and specific accessories for certain postures are hawked at high prices which would make any *yogi* wince. Such a commercialization of Yoga as a fitness and a pastime has also led to the images of pretty contortionists and rugged gymnasts as the Yoga ideals. How often have I heard someone sigh that he or she doesn't have the body for Yoga!

As long as you possess a physical body, then you can perform Yoga. Here we are talking about the spiritual science of Self-Realization. It is a great blessing to possess a precious human body, endowed with the evolutionary mechanisms and tools necessary for transformation and self-realization. You need purchase nothing more.

The physical body is what most of us identify with. It is the only reality which the majority of humanity recognizes, being composed of blood and bones, the nervous system and sense organs.

However, we actually are a five-body complex and are not quite aware of the other four bodies which are made of subtler and subtler matter.

The energy body is just above our normal conscious perception, but can be sensed in recognition of the presence of vitality. It is like an overlay on the physical body energizing and regulating the physical cells. It acts as a channel between the physical world and the higher subtle worlds. Here is where the *chakras* or energy centers are particularly active.

The third body is the emotional body which serves as the mediation between the physical and mental bodies, converting the physical vibrations from the neutral sensations into the "emotionally charged sensations" by adding the qualities of "pleasant" or "unpleasant" or encapsulating it with feelings such as desire or fear. Most physical diseases arise from the emotional or energy bodies.

The mental body is the abode of knowledge and analytical thinking. The "emotionally charged sensations" from the emotional body is processed into perceptual units and fitted into patterns calling forth responses which vibrate back through the emotional body back into the physical realm, causing a physical reaction. This is the realm of thoughts and habit patterns.

The fifth body is the causal body which is both the home of wisdom and of our *karmic* debts. This is the abode of the evolving soul. Higher abstract and intuitive insights arise from here.

The five-body complex exists and functions in different "dimensions" and each is maintained by a different type of energy, from the physical chemical reactions to the subtlest consciousness energy. Each of the bodies has its own energy centers or *chakras* as well as energy channels for controlling and distributing of their own level of energy. Orthodox science only recognizes the centers and channels associated with the physical body, where the cardio-vascular system represents the channels, and the brain and various nerve plexuses correspond to the energy centers. As the *chakras* are activated and awakened, you will become aware of the corresponding dimension of reality, giving you a fuller understanding of the higher dimensions.

Yogis have taught from ancient times that matter was simply a dense form of energy, which in turn is a Continuum of Consciousness.

The Cosmic *Prana,* or universal energy is the life-force or life-breath which permeates all living beings. In the Microcosm, this is represented in each human body as a stored supply of *prana.*

Chakras are energy vortices located along the spinal channel, transformers that change etheric energy to their particular frequency and distribute it to that segment of the physical body which they control. Each *chakra* has its own special function in generating and distributing their forms of *prana* within the nervous system to stimulate glands for rejuvenation.

Nadis are the paths through which *pranic* currents flow – a vast network of astral fibers carrying life force to every cell of the body, essential in maintaining its health and vitality. Yogic tradition speaks of 72,000 *nadis*, centered at the *manipura chakra* or navel center.

Nadis are related to the nerves, but are working at different levels. Nerves carry electrical impulses within the physical body. *Nadis* carry higher vibrational energies to the subtle bodies.

There are three main *nadis* for yogic practice – the *sushumna* or central channel, the *ida* or left moon channel, and *pingala* or right sun channel. They are the basis for the familiar caduceus, which the Greek took from India and has now been used as symbols without understanding.

The *sushumna nadi* is the channel through which *kundalini* should travel, beginning at the base of the spine and runs inside the spinal cord (but of course, not part of the physical spinal cord.) When it reaches a spot at the base of the skull, it divides into two branches. The main branch travels forward through the head to meet the *ajna chakra* or third eye point. This *nadi* is the most important piece of yogic equipment, and is the primary channel for yogic *sadhana* or practice, for evolution and the raising of *kundalini*.

Ida travels from the left side of the *sushumna* and *pingala* on the right side, spiraling around till reaching the left and right nostrils respectively. *Ida* is associated with the moon and female energy, while *pingala* with the sun and male energy.

The Goraksha Samhita has given that there are five manifestations of *prana* in the body:

> In the heart region resides *prana vayu*
> in the anus region *apana vayu*
> in the navel region *samana vayu*
> in the throat region *udana vayu*
> and in the whole body, *vyana vayu* prevails

Prana vayu controls respiration, speech, swallowing, circulation, and body temperature, while *apana vayu* controls digestion, excretion and reproduction, and carries *kundalini* in the *sushumna nadi* (central channel) to unite with *prana vayu*. The *samana vayu* distributes the essential nourishment from food to various parts of the body. *Udana vayu* controls balance and gives strength to the memory and intellect, and carries *kundalini* to the *sahasrara chakra* in the crown of the head.

Health and well-being result when *prana* is freely distributed and properly balanced. Where the flow of *prana* is unbalanced or blocked, mental or physical illness can result. Purification on a mental or etheric level automatically brings about cleansing on the physical level.

Prana enters the body with each inhalation – individual *prana* is absorbed by and through the lungs, the tongue and throat.

The yogi needs to be aware of the subtle bodies and organs, but should not waste time in making an exhaustive study because it is better to spend the time in practice. Knowledge will come through the *sadhana* or practice given by the grace of the Guru.

If you can breathe, then you can practice yoga.

Guidelines for setting up a spiritual practice

One of the first challenges facing a spiritual practitioner is how to get started. Even simple things like which direction to face when meditating and what are best times to do it can bring about doubts and disturbances in the mind.

Generally speaking, any practice or *sadhana* is better than no practice, and it is not necessary in the beginning to be too concerned with facing a particular direction, or even where and when it's being done. Frequent travelers have to practice in hotel rooms and at various time zones. The key is regularity such that at least every twelve hours, one practices - this keeps the momentum of spiritual transformation.

However, as one makes progress on the spiritual path, a certain sensitivity to electromagnetic and other minute phenomena arises. One of these phenomenon that we do not normally consider, is the movement of the earth around its axis. This movement is observed by the rising of the sun in the east and its setting in the west.

It is well known that some people are uncomfortable or even nauseas when sitting in a train facing the opposite direction to its direction of motion. In the same way, it is best to face east when doing one's *sadhana*, as this would place one in the direction of the earth's movement. The effect of facing west may make it more difficult to meditate and increase the time to get comfortably settled into a particular state of consciousness.

If for whatever reason, you cannot face east, then it is recommended by the yogic masters that facing north would be the next best. Facing north aligns the body with the earth's magnetic field.

Of course, when you begin a practice, there are many factors that will impede progress, factors that need to be dealt with and overcome, before we need to consider about which direction to face.

The biggest hurdle is the mental resistance to sitting for the *sadhana* in the first place. It is not easy to get up early in the morning and perform the breathing and meditation techniques that one has learned and must put into practice to derive the benefits from. The best solution to overcome this unwillingness is regularity. Set an achievable goal of doing the practice at the same time in the morning and evening for a period of, let's say, two weeks. Now, this is achievable. It will still take a measure of self-control and determination, but the goal of two weeks should not be a strain. What you will find after two weeks is that you may actually look forward to the two sessions of practice, and it will take less and less effort. It seems strange, but the mind will rebel and come up with all sorts of obstacles, real or imagined, if you make the determination that you will do a consistent practice for the next twenty years, but will provide less resistance if you take it two weeks at a time!

The next hurdle is the physical discomfort. It is difficult to concentrate when the back and knees are aching. The best solution for developing a firm and pain-free sitting posture is the practice of the Hatha Yoga postures. These develop flexibility in the back and knees, among all the other physical and energetic benefits. They also release the causes of discomfort, generally psychosomatic traumas, held in the muscles and joints. Therefore it is necessary to keep a consistent *asana* or physical postures practice.

In the mornings, you can utilize the preliminary movements for fish pose or meenasana – they help to loosen the ankles, knees and hips. In addition, you may want to add an auxiliary pose called the cobbler's pose (*badhakonasana*) that counters backache and sciatica, besides loosening up the knees and hip joints.

The cobbler's pose is practiced in the following way: sit on the floor with a straight, but relaxed back. Straighten the legs forward and then bend the knees and bring the heels close to the groin area as you exhale. Keep breathing normally for a minute or two in this position, then on another exhale, allow the knees to fall towards the sides as far as comfortable, and bring the soles and heels of the feet together. Catch hold of the feet with your hands and utilize micro-movements to lower the knees further to the floor by pressing the thighs with elbow and forearms. Make sure your back is not bent, and breathe normally. Maintain this pose for up to three minutes. Exhale and release the feet, straighten the legs and relax. This pose will, over time, help you to sit comfortably on the floor for longer periods of time.

Another important aid to establishing a consistent practice is to maintain a permanent location for it. Instead of moving around in the house, try to set aside a particular site that doesn't get into anyone's way and is relatively quiet and private. By practicing in that particular place, a spiritual field is gradually built up there. This will help to set up the right conditions for your meditation. The more that you practice in that space, the more it will benefit you. Many people make pilgrimages to sacred places where the great yogis have meditated in the past because they have left a little bit of their spiritual energy in those locations, and it is so much easier to meditate around such sites. Although we are not such great yogis yet, even we can build up enough energy to make our meditation space sacred.

A further refinement to be considered is to keep a practice mat and cushion only for use during your *sadhana* – they should not be used for any other purpose. The mat can be a simple woolen blanket or a wooly sheep-skin, but should not be made of synthetic material. The woolen material helps to insulate the practitioner from the grounding effect of the earth so that the spiritual and *pranic* (life-force) energy can be built up within the body. Another benefit is that the mat will retain some of the energy from your practice and set up a better meditative environment for you.

The space and seat are very helpful to build your very own sacred spot, your own energy vortex. After taking care of the mental, physical and spatial hurdles, you may want to add the refinement of facing east as well.

Certain times of the day or night have been found to be particularly favorable for meditation practice. Generally, the times just before sunrise and just after sunset, that is the twilight times are considered the extremely peaceful periods when the *prana* and consequently the mind is as quiet as it can get.

Traditionally, there is a time about two hours before sunrise, from 3:30 am to 5:30 am that is considered the golden time for spiritual practices. The mind is generally too busy during the afternoon for peaceful meditation.

It is not recommended to practice immediately after meals, as the life-force energy is needed for digestive purposes at the navel center rather than for use at the higher centers.

Yoga of Purification - The Self-Restraints

In common with all of humanity, a spiritual seeker is under the sway of the five senses which are in turn powered by the three cosmic principles or *gunas* of harmony, activity and inertia or *sattva*, *rajas* and *tamas* respectively. Enjoyment of the five senses leads to desires and aversions which in turn lead to fears, anger and lust. In order to attain to the state of a yogic practitioner and qualify for the initiation into the higher practices of Yoga, it is necessary to stabilize and achieve freedom from the control of such passions and emotions.

The yogic practice of self-restraint (*yama*) is an important means of self-purification which prepares the seeker's subtle bodies to be ready for dispassion or detachment (*vairagya*). Normally, the emotional body is filled with desires and strong emotions like fear, anger and lust, while the mental body is preoccupied and dispersed with sensual input and thoughts. By cultivating the *yamas*, one achieves control over the emotional and mental bodies and becomes calm and centered. The energy channels of the energy body are also purified, enabling more energy and life-force to flow through them, as well as to ease the upward movement of the *kundalini* through the *chakras*. Thus, the *yamas* serves a very practical and important function in enabling the goal of spiritual evolution towards Self-realization.

The restraints are given in the scriptures for the purpose of instructing disciples in eluding ignorance and delusion in the world. Ignorance cannot simply come to an end without the help of instruction. Weapons are destroyed by other weapons, dirt cleans dirt and poison cures poison. Ignorance will not go away without self-knowledge and self-knowledge will not dawn until the mind is tamed. When the mind is tamed, one becomes a pathway for the direct experience of higher consciousness from the Divine, the True Self.

Patanjali, one of the eighteen *Siddhas*, wrote very concisely about the integrated science of Yoga. In his *Yoga Sutras*, he divided the path of

Raja Yoga or the "Royal Yoga" into eight limbs, referred to as *Ashtanga* Yoga. In these eight limbs he has given us a template to explore the deeper dimensions of Yoga. They are both the pathways and the unified goal of Self-realization. Just as Yoga "is" both the path or means of Self-realization, as well as the unified state of super-consciousness that results from the practice, so these eight limbs or *anga* are not only practices, but also states of accomplishment, or perfection.

The *yamas* regulate and harmonize the *yogi's* spiritual and moral life, and create the foundation for spiritual practice. They may be difficult to observe at first, and require much conscious effort and exertion of will, but as the yogi develops, their observance becomes not only habitual, but virtually effortless – a function of one's Self-realization.

It is important not to confuse the eight limbs, with 'steps,' which can be practiced consecutively and in isolation. Yoga is integration and wholeness – it is the eight limbs practiced together which constitute Yoga. The eight limbs or *anga* of Yoga are:

1. *yama*: self-restraints through ethical and moral perspective
2. *niyama*: self-discipline through observation of self-realized behavior
3. *asana*: steady posture
4. *pranayama*: control and expansion of the life-energy through the breath
5. *pratyahara*: mind withdrawal from the senses
6. *dharana*: concentration
7. *dhyana*: meditation
8. *samadhi*: super-consciousness or union with the Divine

It is also important to "keep in mind," that meditation without the practice of self-restraint or *yama* would not be considered an effective practice of *Ashtanga* Yoga, or *Kriya Yoga*, which includes the *Ashtanga* model. Merely shifting emphasis from one limb to another does not make one more essential than the other and one should not think that meditation can happen without effort in purifying oneself.

We will focus our attention on the five restraints recommended by Patanjali:

· *Ahimsa* – non-violence
· *Satya* – truth or non-lying
· *Asteya* – non-stealing
· *Brahmacharya* – non-wastage of life-force
· *Aparigraha* – non-attachment

These *yamas* are interrelated with one another, and also with the *niyamas*, or disciplined observances. For example, the *niyama* contentment [*santosha*] will protect one from stealing, that is it helps with the restraint of *asteya*. Besides, meaning 'restraint,' *yama* is also the name of the King of Death, which calls to mind that there must be a dying to ignorance, which is the source of egoism, attachment and repulsion. We are all beset with obstacles and problems as we turn towards the Divine, to reach our highest potential. It is necessary to be constantly examining our thoughts, words and actions with awareness and discrimination so we can come to an understanding of why problems and obstacles occur and by which means they can be avoided. By turning the attention within (Self-awareness) to observe the inner obstacles, thoughts and feelings, the obstructions will be revealed. We will realize what agitates the mind and veils the truth. The *yamas* are to be practiced in thought, word and deed, for example, negative thoughts, harsh words, and physical hurt are all lack of restraint of non-violence or *ahimsa*.

Ahimsa: Non-harming, Non-violence, Non-injury

In the state of divine union, *samadhi*, the yogic sages have unanimously stated that all life is one. If we are to achieve that realization we must affirm that oneness and unity by being kind, compassionate and respectful to all living beings in thought, word and actions. We are advised to refrain from causing or wishing harm, distress or pain to any living being, including ourselves and the world we live in. It would also be necessary to dissuade others from harmful or violent actions - it is not enough to just avoid violence. We should not only refrain from violence against living beings, but in all its manifestations – there can be violence in the way you close a door, cut someone off on the freeway, or even call out a name in anger.

Ahimsa is not merely non-killing or 'Thou shalt not kill.' To live in *ahimsa,* it is important to develop an attitude of perfect harmlessness with positive love and respect for all life, not just in our actions, but in our thoughts and words as well. Our words and thoughts have great power. They can harm others. They can stimulate harmful actions. When we cease to do harm to others, we find that the mind ceases to harbor resentment, envy, anger and fear. Consequently, our mind becomes purified. By cultivating forgiveness we can turn away such feelings, which harm not only others, but ultimately ourselves. With perfection of *ahimsa* one realizes the unity and oneness of all life and attains universal love, peace and harmony. With perfect practice of *ahimsa* one rises above anger, hatred, fear, envy and attachment.

In Yoga-Sutra II.35 Patanjali tells us: "In the presence of one firmly established in non-violence, all hostilities cease." In the process of creating peace within, the *yogi* creates a space where all beings may find peace. The *yogi's* state of mind is a great gift to the world - he or she can help to heal everyone around them. If adversity comes, such a *yogi* welcomes it as an opportunity to heal through it.

Jesus taught in his Sermon on the Mount: "Love those who persecute you." And "if someone strikes you on the cheek, turn to him the other cheek as well." Mahatma Gandhi advocated *ahimsa* as a political and moral practice, and since then others such as Dr. Martin Luther King and Nelson Mandella have used it to advance the civil rights movement. They have demonstrated the power of *ahimsa* not only to transform the individual but society's political and social institutions.

Are there times when one should make an exception, and commit acts of violence? The *Bhagavad Gita,* another important and ancient source of *yogic* inspiration seems to say so. The narrative takes place upon the battlefield of Kurushetra, when Arjuna, the general commanding one army in a civil war, seeing among his enemies many of his relatives, throws down his weapons in disgust and refuses to fight. His charioteer, Krishna persuades him that it is his duty, as a warrior to fight, to protect the *dharma*, the just order of society. The theory of a "just war" is based upon a similar notion that war is justified if one is attacked, in order to preserve the lives of one's family. There is another interpretation that the battle is an allegory of the internal battle each of us has to fight against our negative tendencies, rather than an external battle against other human beings.

It is taken for granted that if an individual is attacked and his life is consequently threatened, it is the duty of that individual to do what is necessary to preserve his own life. However, acts of violence in self-defense should be limited to what is necessary to preserve one's life and those who are aggressed upon, and never committed out of revenge or anger or a desire to inflict suffering on the aggressors. Nevertheless, even righteous violence does not protect one from the consequences of one's actions and there is still negative karmic reaction. Only those whose duty it is to protect society, such as the rulers and soldiers must defend themselves, while others may do so. Those who are intent on Self-Realization must tread the path of total non-violence.

One should study the lives of great souls who have attained perfection in non-violence, such as Buddha, Jesus Christ, Mahatma Gandhi, and St. Francis of Assisi and listen to their words of wisdom. Then we should examine our personal life, work situations and social interactions to observe how we can apply *ahimsa*. Visualize yourself at home, at work, and in social situations and imagine your reaction to certain challenges to non-violence. For example, what would you do, if you are asked to kill a spider on the wall? Or, if someone attacks you verbally or threatens to take something away from you, how would you respond?

Analyze your good and bad tendencies. Consider at the end of each day your conduct, thoughts, words and actions. Be totally honest with yourself and make the necessary changes for improvement.

Give service to others and perform all your actions with love and awareness, offering all the fruits of your action to the Divine. Forgive all those who have 'hurt' you.

Satya: Non-lying, Truthfulness

Truth or *Sat* is one of the aspects of the Divine. As our essential nature is this same Divinity, it is against our true nature to exaggerate, pretend, distort or lie to others, or to manipulate people for our own selfish concerns. When we live in truthfulness we become anchored in the awareness of the Divine.

Why do we lie? It is because of selfishness and the fear of losing one's reputation. However, you can fool some of the people some of the time, but you can never fool your true Self anytime! Honesty with oneself is the first step towards self-improvement.

Can someone achieve any Self-Realization or Self-knowledge by lying to others or to oneself? If we tell lies, we build up a personality which consists of lies and we deceive ourselves. By lying we identify with what we are not and this identification becomes reinforced by the fear of being exposed. The more we lie, the more we are compelled to lie even more to support the previous lies. The more we lie, the further we go from our true Self. Our subconscious becomes filled with the lie and we become more and more preoccupied with its fear-based impulses and reactions. We post-pone the working out of actual *karma,* and create or reinforce new *karmic* consequences. By leaving aside all fiction, all imaginary or unreal things, in mind, speech and action, one quickly discovers what truth is. To speak only what is true is very revealing. So much of what is spoken is so unnecessary, so trivial and unreal. Cultivating silence or speaking only what is edifying and only after reflection, brings great clarity to our minds and relationships. If we are immersed in lying, we will never know the truth or the Divine.

To be truthful means to be radical, to go to the root of things, with unswerving intensity. When we are not truthful for example with ourselves, we allow ourselves to be pushed around by the old programming of our past. Silence is revolutionary. When we are silent, we can become aware of the lies that our mind tries to deceive us with. Doubting our path or the presence of the Absolute, are such lies. Oppose doubt with discernment: distinguish the real, the absolute from the passing show, the ephemeral, the sensual and mental experience.

Faith is truthful if it relies upon the Absolute: that which cannot be apprehended by the mere intellect or senses, but which is ever present, ever conscious, and blissful. The reflections of faith, like love, originate in our soul, that part of the Absolute Truth which partakes of this embodied existence. Faith is not blind. It relies upon a deeper sense, that of the heart, which intuits the Presence. When we must speak from our heart we speak the truth. *Satsang* or sharing of truth in fellowship is a wonderful means of cultivating truth or *satya*. Whether in the presence of one or many, truth expresses itself, uplifts and embraces all who share with utmost sincerity. Sincerity requires us to align our aspiration for the truth, with our thoughts, words and actions. To act in Truth is to act with that intention rather than as a reaction or on impulse. Truth acts correctly or learns from any mistakes. Truth should never be used with the intention to hurt or harm another – it is used compassionately with *ahimsa* in mind. To be truthful is never to be tactless. Thoughtfulness is essential to the usefulness of truth in relationship with others. Only by thinking, speaking and acting in truth will we have peace of mind which is free from fear, anxiety and worry. Only then will truth be respected by people of all persuasions. The power of the universe can be harnessed in the thoughts, words and deeds of those who live in truth.

Truthfulness requires effort at first, because we are in the habit of lying, especially to ourselves. However, with practice it will become easy, especially to ourselves as we notice the wonderful effects of being honest.

In Yoga-Sutra II.36 Patanjali tells us, "To one established in truthfulness, actions and their results depend upon (him)." This means literally that if a person is always truthful, a time will come when all that he says will come true. The *yogi* attains the power to attract whatever he seeks automatically. However, when we indulge in fantasy or half-truths, we dissipate our energy.

In the *Yoga-Bhashya*, an important commentary on the Yoga-Sutras, the sage Vyasa tells us in II.3, that if one speaks at all it should be in order to communicate one's "knowledge and as a service to others, and hence the communication should not be deceitful, erroneous, or barren."

In the Bible (Psalm 46:10) it says: "Be still and know that I am God." By understanding this simple verse we begin to find inner communion with the Divine, which speaks to our minds, fills our hearts with truth and inspiration when our consciousness is attuned to the inner silence. When the mind is silent, energy slowly gathers. Thought and egoic preoccupations scatter the energy. When the mind is still, it reflects life accurately, without distortion.

Introspection and self-observation can take place when the mind is still and becomes aware of the different types of thoughts, desires, longings and fears.

Observe every thought and feeling as it arises in the mind, being aware of its cause, content and meaning. By observing your thoughts like this, suppressed experiences in the unconsciousness mind start to unfold themselves. Tremendous energy is released while unburdening the unconscious mind of all conflict. After some time of practice the mind will experience stillness in which there is no observer or observed. Awareness of silence and peace is stabilized in truth, as delusions and illusions of the mind are forsaken.

Make a personal commitment to express truth in your life as a means to Self-Realization, as a blessing to every person you meet, without hurt or harm. Express truth in thought, word and deed to all living beings. Live in truth, love and harmony, and share it with others.

Be aware of your thoughts, when you interact at home, in the office or social activities. Only speak those words which are truthful. Before you speak, examine your thoughts to determine if they are selfish or harmful. Will they cause distress to someone? Your thoughts, words and actions should be in harmony with each other and to truth.

Understand yourself. Be ready to admit your faults and errors without feelings of guilt or sorrow. This is the first step to self improvement. Search out truths about yourself on all levels, including your likes and dislikes, without being judgmental or prejudiced.

Develop an attitude of truthfulness. Always recognize and accept the state of things and circumstances as they are and work with what is.

Visualize yourself in different situations where truth is an issue, and analyze your possible reactions in the light of the Divine. Will you tell a lie to save someone from death? What about lying to ensure a murderer is put away from harming others?

Asteya: Non-stealing

Asteya means to avoid stealing, or appropriating things which belong to another. Stealing may take many forms, aside from the obvious types of theft such as shoplifting, cheating on a tax return, overcharging a customer, not paying a debt or bankruptcy. Plagiarism, cheating on examinations and infidelity are other forms of stealing. Stealing often occurs on a subtle level when we steal people's time, affections, emotions, attention, ideas and thoughts. There are some who perform these acts of subtle stealing consciously, while others do them subconsciously out of a need to win attention and fame for themselves. Question yourself: At work do you ever take credit for an accomplishment realized by a subordinate? Do you ever blame others for your own mistakes?

Regardless of what is being stolen, the primary cause for stealing is a lack of contentment, which leads to greed and desire, manifesting as insecurity, selfishness, greed, and poverty consciousness. Stealing engulfs our consciousness with darkness, wherein we fail to see our essential unity. It closes our hearts, strengthens egoistic tendencies and drives us away from the path to Self-realization. By indulging in stealing we give up our power of self-control and strengthen the hold that negative forces may have upon us. Our consciousness contracts around whatever the ego dangles before it, insisting that our happiness depends upon it.

When we are discontent with the present, desire keeps one continually looking to the future for one's fulfillment, instead of realizing that perfection is attainable here and now. To try to gain satisfaction by fulfilling the endless desires that arise in the mind is an utterly futile endeavor, which only causes unhappiness and sorrow. Desire arises from the ego or "I" consciousness from the thoughts of 'I want,' 'I need,' or 'I must have.' In the experience of the great sages, contentment arises only from permanent happiness and joy, permanent peace, and love, and not in the satisfaction of passing desires. To experience this we must look within, it cannot be found outside of ourselves. The mind is constantly turning outward, because it believes that fulfillment lies in the external world. However, as Jesus taught: 'The Kingdom of God is within you" (Luke 17:2), and once you attain love, joy and peace from within, it will also come to you from without.

Just as we forget our "I" during deep sleep, we forget our true Self or Identity to the Divine, during our waking state. It is through this forgetfulness of our true identity and our relationship to the Divine that we feel lost, experience unhappiness and live in poverty consciousness.

Until we have a conscious awareness of the Divine's presence within, it cannot bear fruit in our experience. When we are attuned and surrendered to the Divine, we become consciously aware, and open to the universe, which provides all that we need. We derive everything from Divine Consciousness and we are all a part of the Consciousness.

Eliminate all negative thoughts of lack, poverty and failure from your mind. Live from within by attuning your will with the Divine Will, and let Divine Wisdom be your guide in everything. Stealing shows a distrust of the intimate relationship with the Divine. We must realize that every breath we take is by Divine grace. The Divine is the source and cause of all. The Divine rained manna from the skies to feed the hungry people because Moses trusted in the Divine.

Is it right to steal a loaf of bread to feed a dying child? We can always rationalize or justify certain actions, but even such a kind action is a transgression that has to be held accountable. Of course, it may be balanced on the scales of *karma,* by the compassion of saving a life, and yet it is a consequence of a lesser consciousness. In higher consciousness and trust in the Divine, the Divine compassion will supply the child with food somehow. It is also important to realize that stealing can cause the breaking of other *yamas.* If we try to conceal a theft, we would lie, or even resort to violence. This is not an injunction for inaction in the face of another's need. As long as we are mired in lesser consciousness, it is better to take action to help another, even if it means transgressing a self-restraint such as non-stealing.

In his Yoga-sutra II.37 Patanjali tells us that, "Wealth comes to all established in non-stealing." Stealing occurs when we desire something that does not belong to us, and then one acts upon that desire. If instead, we give, we allow the universe to give us more, and to work through us. Ultimately we must realize that we are not the doer and cease to take credit for things accomplished. Cease to misappropriate or steal the credit. Once we are established in non-stealing, we will strive to do the work, or to work things out with a lot of care, without tension, without expectation of a return. All wealth comes with selflessness. We are awarded with the four things that make us truly wealthy: equality, peace, spiritual ease in all circumstances and joy and laughter of the soul.

Channel all your desires into one desire – the desire for Self-realization. Realize and understand that it is the desire or need for something apart from the Divine that keeps us separate from the Universal Source of All.

It is false to believe that we can be satisfied with something outside of ourselves, other than the presence and the Power of God. When you hold the desire for union with the Divine, Yoga, above all other desires, then other desires will subside.

Develop a consciousness of abundance and you will receive freely from the universal supply. Attune your will to the Divine Will. Realize that if you have any sense of lack, it is because your thoughts, ideas and beliefs have conditioned your mind to hold these limitations. Turn your thoughts from lack and limitation, to the belief in the inevitable operation of God working for you in abundance.

Examine your life and relationships and eliminate all non-essential things and activities. You may wish to consider minimizing your contacts with egocentric people who have conflicting and negative patterns of thought to your spiritual views on life.

Practice *Karma Yoga* by giving service to other, with no expectation of reward. This awakens compassion and takes attention away from our personal feelings of lack. When we consciously serve and give from our heart, we attract the down-flow of Divine grace into our lives.

Brahmacharya: Non-sensuality, chastity, non-wastage of life-force

Brahmacharya is consciousness anchored in the Divine. It is mind ever turned toward the Divine. It is the state of Yoga or ecstatic union with the Source of All. In Yoga, *brahmacharya* becomes effortless. However, until Yoga is achieved, continuous effort is necessary to turn our thoughts, words and actions towards the Divine.

In ancient India, most saints and *yogis* were householders. They would bring up families, performing their duties to society, while continuing their practice of Yoga and leading a spiritual life. To them, there was no conflict between sex and God. Asceticism and celibacy were temporary periods of intense practice, but not necessarily a way of life, until monastic Buddhism entered into the Indian religious tradition.

Sexuality is regarded as an obstacle to spiritual life, in the Judeo-Christian religions and this has falsely programmed feelings of guilt, shame and sin, in the modern consciousness, towards something the Divine has created for the purposes of procreation and creativity.

Still, it remains that most people interpret *brahmacharya* as only restraint of sexual impulses or celibacy, rather than as a sublimation of all passions through deeper emotions of loving, kindness and affection. If *brahmacharya* only meant celibacy then married people who wanted children would not be able to practice Yoga. It is because *brahmacharya* has a wider meaning than the restraint of the sexual impulse, that there have been so many householder saints with children. The greatest *yogis* and *rishis* of all times, such as Vashista and Yagnavalkya were householders, and in recent times, there was Lahiri Mahasaya who, in 1861, was initiated into the ancient techniques of Kriya Yoga in the Himalayas, by the immortal master Mahavatar Babaji. Lahiri Mahasaya and his wife had five children born to them, some years after Lahiri's initiation by Babaji.

Although *brahmacharya* should be practiced at all levels of energy usage, it is necessary that in these days, where sexual excitation is rampant in all walks of life, and sexual frustration is at all time highs, that we should first examine the sexual perspective above all others. *Brahmacharya* does include chastity and does involve detachment from sexual fantasies. For fantasizing about sex, or indulging in lustful feelings dissipates and disperses the mind, just as the physical acts of sex cause the loss of vital force. In Yoga-Sutra II.38 Patanjali tells us that "By one established in chastity, vigor is gained." The cultivation of *brahmacharya* will enable us to sublimate vital energy to awaken the higher centers of consciousness, and to turn the consciousness away from fleeting sense sensations and towards the ultimate inner source of joy.

Brahmacharya is not really the abandonment of sex, but the placement of sex within a spiritual perspective. The question is not, 'Shall I renounce sex, marriage and social responsibility for a life of spiritual practice?' but 'What is my right relationship to them?' It is the same question, whether one is following the householder's path or the path of renunciation. Some are attached to sexual indulgence, making sex into an addiction, as they strive towards ever more and stronger orgasms. The mind becomes obsessed with sex, causing undue tension. Excessive indulgence in sexuality leads only to sorrow and pain. The mind is agitated while the intellect is impaired and unable to discriminate. Physical radiance and magnetism decreases with loses of sexual energy and vitality. Boredom, depression and discontent sets in, as in all obsessions and addictions. From a spiritual or moral perspective, a sexual relationship should be based on commitment to one person. There has to be commitment and loving concern for each other to make the relationship meaningful. Sexuality is not just a toy provided for our physical pleasures divorced from responsibility and care. A relationship for the purpose of ego-gratification through the senses is meaningless. For a true spiritual relationship to take form, sex for self-gratification must end. Love can express itself naturally and spiritually in joyful sexual intimacy.

It must be also noted here that repression or denial can be just as harmful as over-indulgence – both are ego-centric and can make the mind dull, losing its sensitivity and awareness. There is no lasting joy in either indulgence or repression. We continue to see that monastics, *yogis* or priests, who try to deny their sexual natures, without the proper perspectives and methods of practice, eventually harm themselves and others as they secretly try to gratify their perverted, rather than sublimated natures. This is amply demonstrated by the recent scandals involving Catholic Priests.

It is instructive to remember the words of Krishna, in counseling moderation in all things:

> *Yoga is not for those who eat too much, or too little, nor for those who sleep too much or too little. It is for those who are moderate in eating, sleeping, wakefulness, recreation and all actions, that yoga will bring an end to all sorrows. Those who have learned to discipline their minds and remain calmly established in the Self, free from attachment to all desires, attain to the state of union.*

We should practice regular meditation to overcome egocentric thoughts and emotions, and to hold everyone in respect as of equally divine nature. Such meditation will turn the energy inwards and upwards to higher centers of awareness. The proper practice of Yoga and meditation transforms the sexual energy (semen or ovum on the physical level) into spiritual or subtle energy (*ojas*) by directing and channeling it upwards towards the higher energy centers, or *chakras*, through the subtle pathway in the spine called the *sushmna nadi*.

When you are following a spiritual path and are not married or in a sexual relationship, you will find Yoga postures and practices helpful in conserving and transforming the sexual energy on the physical level into *ojas* on the spiritual level. Men lose more of the vital fluid during the sexual act than the women do, but both have vital fluids whose loss due to excessive sexual indulgence causes loss of vitality and unsteadiness of *prana* in the body. Those people who are married or in a sexual relationship will benefit from these practices, as they have rejuvenating and toning effects on the sex centers, glands, nerves, and body systems, promoting longevity and vitality.

One should practice self-enquiry as follows: Am I able to keep God in my heart, mind, and body when I am having a sexual experience? Am I able to make love as an offering to the Divine? Am I able to remain as the Seer in relation with the Seen? Am I able to see my partner as an embodiment of the Divine?

Only by understanding the nature of desires can we prevent them. A regular practice of Self-enquiry eventually releases us from our selfish thoughts and our ego will weaken. When we are calmly centered within, in a state of attentive awareness at all times, free from conflict, our energy is conserved. By turning the mind inward to investigate its own source and nature, it is illuminated by the Self. When the mind is turned outward and lost in desires and attachments, our energy is wasted and our true eternal nature is ignored. We forget our true Self through identification with the body, mind and ego. We experience happiness and unhappiness, pleasure and pain because the body and mind are ever in the midst of change. That which changes cannot be real, only that which is permanent and eternal is real.

Aparigraha: Non-attachment, Non-greed

The Sanskrit word *apara* means "of another" and *agraha* means "to crave for." Therefore, *aparigraha* is usually translated as "without craving for that which belongs to another." However, in a deeper sense it means not to be craving for the "unreal," the "not-self" – it is non-attachment to everything that is not the True Self.
We receive Divine Grace in greater abundance, when we open and attune ourselves to the Divine Will. With faith in, and understanding of Divine Grace, one can live a more fulfilling life.

In Light of Kriya Yoga

Non-greed is not only resisting the temptation to covet what belongs to others, but also means non-attachment even to one's own possessions, as well as not to hoard or accumulate unnecessary amounts of something. It is instructive to remind ourselves that, we come into this world with nothing and we depart with nothing. Our true security is in the Divine which is always with us, within our hearts. When we let the Divine move into every area of our life, the spirit of truth and love becomes the foundation of our security.

It is ignorance that leads us to a mistaken sense of duality, which gives rise to a desire to experience, from which egoism or "I-sense" takes root. The ego principle gives rise to greed, insecurity and attachment. When we act from attachment we try to manipulate situations and other people out of fear of losing the desired object. Subjected to selfish desires, fear and greed, we live an insecure life. Greed arises when the mind clings to the mistaken belief concerning where one's security is derived from as in, "I will die without that person!" or "My security comes from being in this job, owning this house and being with my family." In this way, we develop a false basis for our security by placing our power in such transitory things or by accumulating more possessions than we actually need.

How much is too much in terms of possessions? In a society where self-worth is usually measured in terms of wealth, the question may seem odd. But for those of us who seek to align all of our values with our spiritual life, the question is immensely important. The *Bhagavad Gita* IV.21 calls for the abandonment of all possessions. This has inspired a movement of "renunciation" of the world, particularly in the Indian Hindu and Buddhist traditions. Jesus admonished his disciples in parables concerning the birds that neither sow nor reap, but are provided for by the Lord. He says not to lay up treasures on earth but in heaven. However, other scriptural authorities, such as the *Bhagavata-Puranam* III.28.4 advocate a much more moderate approach to greedlessness: "possess as much as is necessary."

The consideration from the *siddhas* perspective is that there is nothing inherently wrong with material possessions, as long as they do not possess the possessor! That is, when one becomes attached to one's stuff, one suffers immediately, and fails to recognize the true source of joy and well being: one's own inner Self. Therefore, the *yogi* experiences equanimity in all gains or loses. When unexpected losses occur or threaten, one remembers, "Who loses?" And the answer: "No one." For, the *yogi,* there is never any gain or loss, for the *yogi* does not identify with the body-mind, but with that infinite and eternal Being, the all blissful Self. For the *yogi,* everything is transitory - why allow yourself to indulge in thoughts of gain or loss?

Think of something that you really like or want at this moment. "Why do you want it?" "Can you live without it?" "How much of it do you need?" As you continue in this way, repeat with other objects of desire and greed. In this way, the heart is purified.

Visualize yourself getting unlimited amounts of what you crave. This can be elaborated as you spend time imagining yourself enjoying and reveling in the midst of your possessions. "How do you feel?" "Are you satisfied?" "Do you want more?" "Do you feel fear of losing it all?" "Do you fear other people may steal from you?" Now see yourself stripped of everything that you have? "How do you feel now?"

Meditate regularly to cleanse your subconscious mind. Release attachment to objects, relationships, bad habits, negative attitudes and conditionings which block your experience of truth. Let Divine Wisdom and grace be your guide, and strength.

When there is hatred, resentment, anger, jealousy or violence toward another, the mind and breath become unsteady. Abandon all destructive and negative thoughts by cultivating the opposite, positive qualities of love, compassion, patience, tolerance, and kindness. In addition, one should practice breathing techniques so that the length of the inhalation and the exhalation are of equal duration, cultivating calmness in the breath, mind and *prana.*

While the *yamas* are listed as the first of the eight limbs of *Ashtanga* Yoga, they are not merely preliminary. They also denote the qualities of one who has become a master of Yoga, one who is Self-realized. It is relatively easy to have spiritual experiences, but until and unless one becomes purified of the lower tendencies of human nature, there will be no lasting state of Self-realization, no true freedom, no enlightenment. While the resistance of our ordinary human nature, based upon an egoistic perspective will undoubtedly require sustained effort to observe the *yamas* for many years, they will eventually become effortless, as one identifies more and more with what one is and lets go of what one is not. Thus, the *yamas* are an integral part of the practice of Yoga, and any attempt to ignore them leads only to ignoring our true Self.

note: the yamas form the most important step towards the path of spiritual evolution and so I've given a longer treatment of this topic and have also written a book called Yoga of Purification and Transformation, about the yamas and niyamas

Yoga of Transformation - Niyama

While the five-fold *yama* or self-restraints purify the mind, we must understand *yogic* physiology in order to place the mind in its proper perspective. What is normally called the mind is properly termed *manas* and is a mode of the mental body, used effectively for dealing with the world of the five senses, and as such is a barrier to higher consciousness. *Manas* is a fine tool for what it is meant to do, but because of the dominance of another mode of the mind called "I-ness" or *ahamkara*, it has malfunctioned and can no longer provide an accurate representation of the world.

Ahamkara or ego which serves the function of a temporary separation of identity from the true Self is useful for an unlimited consciousness to experience limitations. However, when *ahamkara* is dominant, there is a loss of the connection to the unlimited consciousness, and the mind or *manas* can only experience the world in an egocentric miasma of confusion, doubt and fear. The sensory images from *manas* are filtered through *ahamkara*, resulting in likes and dislikes, possessiveness, and desires. Through the conscientious practice of the five self-restraints of *yama*, the grip of "I-ness" is dislodged and *manas* is freed to experience the world as it is.

The spiritual seeker first must begin the practice of the self-restraints and remove the barrier of the mind before Self-realization can be achieved. However, the aspiring *yogi* need not wait to begin practice of the five-fold self-discipline of the *niyama*.

There is a higher mode of consciousness beyond the mind and the "I-ness". It is called *buddhi* or "light of wisdom" or the "clear mind of pure consciousness". There is no good English translation for *buddhi*, and the normal one used is intellect which is inadequate, as is discriminatory mind.

The self-discipline of *niyama* lets the light of *buddhi* shine through the purified *manas*, such that the spiritual aspirant begins to see reality as it is. As the *buddhi* brings light to the darkness of ignorance, the practice of *yama* is perfected and requires less and less effort until it becomes effortless.

By the practice of purifying the body and mind [*saucha*] and cultivating contentment [*santosha*], one is able to loosen the hold of the ego. Then through the practice of self-study [*svadyaya*] and surrender to the Divine [*ishvar pranidhana*], the light of *buddhi* is allowed to shine forth and illuminate the seeker's life.

> *Shaucha (purity), santosha (contentment), tapas (austerity), svadyaya (self- study), and Ishvara pranidhana (surrender to the Divine) constitute the self-observances.*
> Yoga Sutras 2:32

Shaucha (purity) is cleanliness of the body and purity of the mind. As the mind and body are interdependent, purification of the body is a means of controlling the mind. By observing cleanliness one becomes less attached to one's own body. When purity is perfected one gains control of the senses and becomes cheerful, one-pointed, and fit for Self-realization.

Santosha (contentment) is not just a passive state of mind. It is a virtue to be actively cultivated in order to free the mind from the effects of pleasure and pain. When contentment is perfected, one becomes desire-less and attains unexcelled happiness.

Tapas (austerity) is literally, "to burn" and implies the burning of all desires by means of discipline, purification, and penance. Fasting, enduring heat or cold, and observing silence are examples of gross methods of *tapas*. Any form of giving up desires is *tapas*. *Pranayama* (breath expansion and control) is considered to be the highest austerity, as it requires great restraint of the normal, life-giving breath. When austerity is perfected one achieves control over the body and the senses. In a sense all techniques of Yoga can be considered as forms of *tapas*. *Svadhyaya* (self-study) includes all Self-inquiry, study of scriptures, *satsang* (spiritual meetings), and *japa* (repetition) of *Om*, with the aim of attaining liberation. Studying the inspirational and holy literature, as well as studying the lives and teachings of saints are helpful in the beginning. Self-inquiry is done by reflecting deeply on the question, "Who am I?" *Satsang* is association with spiritually oriented people and places. As *Om* is the origin of all *mantras* (sacred sounds or words), the *japa* of *Om* may be extended to include any *mantras* used for liberation. Through *svadhyaya* one can contact the form of the Divine with whom one desires to have a deeper relationship.

Ishvarapranidhana (surrender to Divine) is the recognition that the limited, ego-self is an illusion. It is the channeling of energies toward the realization of truth, or the Divine. One who sees the Self in all beings and who has surrendered the ego of being the "doer" is the true practitioner of *Ishvarapranidhana*. Perfection of *this niyama* brings success in *samadhi* or super-consciousness.

Consider how each of the *niyama* may relate to your life at this time. How do you deal with purity of body or mind? Bathing has both physical and subtle effects and should be done every day. Are you pursuing some kind of self-study? Is this something that appeals to you?

Let us take *santosha* or contentment and consider this more, since it is the source of happiness. Is there something pro-active that you can do to increase you level of contentment? Have you been thinking that contentment was a future state that will "happen" after some sort of spiritual epiphany?

Contentment is an active state which can be cultivated by practicing mindfulness and constant self-awareness in order to stay in the present – the here and now.

Without attentive awareness and alertness, our consciousness becomes clouded, we become sleepy and our senses lose their sensitivity and become dull. When our attention and sensitivity are sharpened and heightened with awareness, our perception becomes clear. In this state of observation we are able to perceive and recognize those limiting conditions and can understand why the mind is distracted and inattentive. In unbroken, clear awareness we can de-condition and de-hypnotize the mind of its subconscious grasping after some future gratification of desires.

Self-awareness begins with you here and now in this moment, in every moment of your life. When you live every moment in awareness, you will experience the Eternal as a living reality. The average person only uses a tiny fraction of awareness in his or her everyday living. We go from one day to the next throughout life in a state of distraction, unawareness and restlessness. We are sleeping with our eyes open, unaware of the beauty around us.

In the conditioned state of mind we are subject to our subconscious motives, and therefore our perceptions are distorted. We are not even aware or mindful when eating our meals or listening when someone is talking to us. How often do people leave water running from a tap, or forget to switch a light or heater off before going out. These may seem like inconsequential small activities in one's life, but the way to self-realization requires the sensitivity, awareness, care and attention to all that we do in thought, word and action - no matter how small it may seem. We need to live each moment of our life completely, carefully observing all the details with constant awareness and attention.

The sages constantly remind us that it does not matter how long you have been sitting in the dark … when light is brought in, the darkness disappears. It is our responsibility to awake in the light, to consciously know our true nature and reality as the Self. It is through mastery of our mind, body and senses that we can direct our lives intelligently and super-consciously, expressing our selves in a balanced and fulfilling way on all levels of our being.

Self-knowledge is the awareness of the immortal reality within us, which sets us free from the bondage of ignorance, the cause of all our sorrows. This knowledge and awareness, which is the Self, is here and now, always. It has never ceased to be, and so is not a goal that we have to search for.

There is no mystery to it. All we need to do is remove the obstacles, dispelling the ignorance that obscures the Self as knowledge. The sun is always shining, but when it is obscured by dark clouds we do not see it. When the clouds disperse then the sun becomes visible and the light shines.

The past is gone and cannot be changed, while the future is not yet and cannot be known – all we have is the present. Yet we brood about the past and fear for the future, forgetting to live in the present. Let us resolve to be mindful and live life in the Here and Now.

Postural Integration

The yogic postures or *asanas* which are the most frequently appearing images for the whole scientific art of Yoga these days do serve important purposes. They form the third step or *pada* of Ashtanga Yoga or the eightfold path mentioned by the Patanjali in his Yoga Sutras.

Externally, the postures serve to keep the body flexible through the bending and stretching movements and the holding of specific poses for limited time. The pressures on different parts of the body help to remove toxins from the internal organs and keep the body healthy. There are sitting and standing poses which help to develop firmness and stability of the body. If the body is fidgety or stiff, then it is not possible to remain in a stable meditative pose. The development of a stable meditative pose is a necessity for the development of a stable and meditative mind.

> *Asanas are treated in the first because they form the first part of Hatha Yoga. Their purpose is to make one firm, free from diseases and light of limb.*
> Hatha Yoga Pradipika 1.17

Besides the physical benefits of the postures, there are certain internal transformations which can occur when additional factors are brought to play. These factors and transformations depend on the interdependence of the five bodies possessed by human beings. The five bodies are formed from different grades of matter, from the gross physical body to the finest subtle causal body. In between are the energy, emotional and mental bodies. The basic premise is that something done to the physical body has a ripple effect in all the other bodies.

It is because of the interdependence of the five bodies that *mudras* can work. When a yogi touches the tip of his thumb with the tip of the index finger, it forms what is called the *chin mudra*, extremely conducive to developing the attitude of self-control. It works because, by connecting the nerves at the tip of the two fingers, certain other connections are made in the energy, emotional and mental bodies which produce the attitude of self-control.

Postures can be used to attain a balanced mind – a balance between the rational faculty and the intuitive faculty. Yoga is all about integration, balance and harmony. When a person is too rational and lack the intuitive and creative aspects or it maybe the other way around, she may be too intuitive and lack analytical ability, then that person is unbalanced, non-integrated and so using only a portion of her potential.

People mistake the mind with the brain. The brain is only the physical expression of the mind, which is in the mental body. The brain has two portions, the left brain for rational expression and the right brain for intuitive expression. The right brain is connected to the left side of the body and the left brain is connected to the right side of the body. When one balances the left and right sides of the body, one can balance the left and right sides of the brain, and in turn the rational and intuitive faculties in the mental body.

As an illustration on how seemingly minor details can significantly change the effect of postures, we can examine one of the most commonly recommended sitting postures for spiritual practitioners, the *siddhasana* or pose of perfection. In the Hatha Yoga Pradipika, it is specified that the left heel is touching the perineum. This has the effect of connecting the left side of the body or the right brain to the first *chakra* or energy center, where *kundalini*, the personal aspect of the primordial cosmic creative matrix (*shakti*) resides.

> *Press firmly the heel of the left foot against the perineum and the right heel above the male organ. With the chin pressing on the chest, one should sit tight, having restrained the senses and gaze steadily at the space between the*

eyebrows. This is called siddhasana, the opener of the door to liberation.

Hatha Yoga Pradipika 1.37

The effect of connecting the left heel is to promote the intuitive, creative and passive mind, the so-called "female" side. This is especially good for men, as they tend to be left brained and so it would balance their polarity. However, women might wish to balance their right side by activating their right heel. In the Siva Samhita, which heel to use is not specified and it is up to the teacher to guide the students according to their natures - man who has a passive nature might need to balance their active side by using the right heel rather then use the left, or a woman might need to activate her creative side with the left heel.

The siddhasana that gives success to the practitioner is as follows – pressing with care by the heel the yoni (perineum in men), the yogi should place the other heel on the lingam (male organ), and fix his gaze upwards on the space between the eyebrows. He should remain steady and restrain his senses.

Siva Samhita 3.85

To complicate matters further, another authoritative text, the Gheranda Samhita, tells the practitioner to place the heel under the anal sphincter, in effect placing sitting on the heel. This accomplishes effect of closing one of the doors through which life-force energy or *prana* leaks out of the body. This is giving a different effect and is a variation of the *siddhasana* mentioned in the other two texts.

The practitioner who has subdued his passions, having placed one heel at the anal aperture should keep the other heel on the root of the generative organ. He should then rest his chin upon the chest and with a straight back, gaze at the spot between the two eyebrows. This is called siddhasana which leads to emancipation.

Gheranda Samhita 2.7

All three texts agree that the other heel should be placed against the sexual organs. This serves two purposes, first it completes the energy circuit with the first heel, and second, it closes another door through which the body leaks out life-force. The position above the sex organs is a connection to the location on the spine where the second energy *chakra* is co-located (not in the physical body, but in the energy body.)

The chin resting on the chest is called the chin-lock and helps to pull life-force energy to stimulate the third-eye or sixth energy *chakra*. It also keeps energy from flowing down from the higher centers to the lower centers. Gazing at the spot between the eyebrows stimulates the third-eye center.

It is also worth mentioning that the position of the hands is not given in the texts, as well as certain other important considerations. These texts were written down as notes for those who have been given direct instruction form qualified teachers, and were meant to jog the memory, but were not detailed or exhaustive in their content. In fact, it is quite possible that instead of using encryption, certain key details were omitted to prevent unauthorized use. It is never advisable to practice from books alone.

Breathe Like your Life Depends on It

Pranayama is the Sanskrit term for the *yogic* science and art of breathing. It is formed from two root words *prana* and *ayama*. *Prana* means a "subtle life-force" which gives energy to the mind and body, and *ayama* signifies the voluntary effort to control, direct and expand this *prana*.

Pranayama is both a physical process of regulating the breath voluntarily as well as the subtle expansion of the *prana*. It is the union of the individual *prana* with the Universal *Prana*, and forms an integral part of *Yoga*, the science of self-realization.

The first purpose of *pranayama* is to improve the health and prolong the life of the body, in order that the aspiring *yogi* can have a better life and longer time to perfect his practice and reach his goal.

The second purpose is to purify the subtle energy channels, the *nadis*, in the subtle energy body called the *pranamayakosa*, in order to allow *prana* to flow into the central *nadi*, called *sushumna*.

The third purpose is as a lead-in for meditation or *dhyana*, as mental fluctuations are eliminated with the balancing of *prana*.

The basic parts or movements of *pranayama* are *puraka* (inhalation), *rechaka* (exhalation) and *kumbhaka* (retention of the breath).

> *Inhalation, exhalation, and retention both ways;*
> *The Science of Breath thus consisting – they know not.*
> *They who know the Science of Breath*
> *Are destined to spurn the god of death.*
> Tirumundirum 571

During deep meditation the breath naturally becomes suspended for a short period of time, and during this interval, there is no sense of time;

the mind is still, and in that deep peace, there is joy or bliss. The *yogic* explanation of this phenomenon is that it is the breath (or the movement of *prana*) that enables your mind to think. When this is suspended, then the mind loses its fuel, and so it is no longer distracted, and becomes very still.

> *Let prana merge in mind*
> *And together the two be stilled*
> *Then no more shall birth and death be;*
> Tirumundirum 567

The stilling of breath is a key parameter in most of the major breathing techniques, and this has led to a lot of controversy on how and when breath retention should be practiced. There are four types of *kumbhaka* or retention of breath mentioned by *Patanjali* in his *Yoga Sutras*:

- *Bahya kumbhaka* (external breath retention): a pause after a very slow and prolonged exhalation.
- *Abhyantara kumbhaka* (internal breath retention): a pause after a deep, prolonged inhalation.
- *Stambha kumbhaka* (middle breath retention): a prolonged pause in between the inhalation and exhalation.
- *Kevala kumbhaka* (spontaneous retention): this is experienced by the practitioner at any time without any effort. It comes automatically after prolonged practice of *pranayama*.

Although the *Yoga Sutras* do not give any *pranayama* techniques or describe any of the methods of breath retention, some general principles are given:

> *The variations in Pranayama are external, internal or suspended. The interval is regulated by place, duration and number, and becomes progressively prolonged and subtle. The fourth type is the spontaneous suspension of*

the breath that occurs while concentrating on something external or internal.
                                                    Yoga Sutras 2:50,51

In the above *Sutras, Patanjali* introduced the factors that can be controlled during the breath retention interval - place refers to where the breath is held (external, internal or suspended). Duration refers to the duration of the breath retention and number means the ratio between inhalation, retention and exhalation of the breath

Hatha Yoga texts, such as the *Hatha Yoga Pradipika* focus primarily on the forceful application of *kumbhaka*, rather than on *kevala*, for the simple reason that there are no specific techniques for *kevala*, and it normally takes prolonged practice to achieve the latter, while the effects of forceful breath retention can be quick. However, the unsupervised and indiscriminate practice of such forced breath retention can be dangerous to the physical and mental health of the practitioner. *Pranayama* can eradicate all diseases if properly practiced, but if done improperly, may cause aggravation. (Hatha Yoga Pradipika 2.16**)**

A competent guide, common sense and the correct application of the *bandhas* or muscular locks are essential factors for the success in practicing forced *kumbhaka*. It must also be borne in mind that even in Hatha Yoga, the goal of *pranayama* is to achieve the state of *kevala*.

There is a lot of misunderstanding about the practice of breath retention or holding of breath, due to the popularization of advanced *Yogic* texts, which appear to promote this practice indiscriminately. In general, holding of breath can put a stress on your heart and circulatory system, elevating the blood pressure several times above normal, which can result in ruptured blood vessels or a stroke.

What may not be clear from books is that beginners in *Yoga* are not taught the holding of breath, until they have had years of practice in strengthening the body, circulatory system and nervous systems, and only after authorization and personal supervision from their teachers. When holding of breath is taught, it should always be accompanied by the practice of the muscular locks or *bandhas*.

It is my personal experience and observation, that most breathing techniques do not require the active and forced breath retention, but will over time, increase the natural pause between the inhaled breath and the exhaled breath. This natural pause does not put a strain on the heart.

All the *pranayama* techniques can be practiced without forced holding of breath and can encourage the spontaneous stilling of breath.

The Yogic Benefits of Pranayama

The great *Siddha* or perfected being called *Tirumoolar* has given us the manifold benefits of *pranayama*, in his great text of yoga, called the Tirumandirum:

- Longevity of the body is gained by breath control. By controlling inhalation and exhalation of the breath, and centering of the mind, the body is preserved. The physical body has nine openings: two eyes, two nostrils, two ears, mouth, genital opening, and anal opening. The nine-windowed house is the vehicle of the soul and can be kept for a long time by the proper practice of *pranayama*.

- The mind is tamed by breath control

  What though you wake and pray?
  They who control breath in measure ordained,
  Will sure imprison mind-monkey
  within the body fortress.
                    Tirumandirum 595

The mind has been likened by *Swami Vivekenanda*, to a drunken monkey stung by the bee of passion.... almost impossible to tame, and control.

Patanjali has also given emphasis to the benefit of mental control through the breath in his Yoga Sutras 2:52-3: The attainment of *pranayama* removes mental darkness and ignorance, which veils the inner Light of the soul......And the mind attains the power to concentrate.

When the breath is controlled, the mind becomes still, and concentration or one-pointedness arises.

- Purification of the Energy and Physical Bodies

  The breath is used to flush the ida and pingala
  By pranayama, the heart gets purified,
  And the body becomes impervious even to fire.
                              Tirumandirum 726

  The *ida* and *pingala* are two *nadis* or energy channels which transport *prana* or life-force in the Energy Body, analogous to blood vessels which transport oxygen to the organs in the Physical Body. By the purification of the Energy and Physical Bodies, the *prana* or healing life-force can travel unobstructed.

- Breath control leads to *Samadhi* or the ecstatic state of Yoga

  When prana course through the adharas six
  Then will nectar be;
  When prana reaches the seventh center of the Sun
  And further onward to the eighth center of the Moon;
  In the ninth center prana attains samadhi.
                              Tirumandirum 703

The *adharas* are also called *chakras* or wheels of energy, and are the localized energy centers in the Energy Body. This verse describes the process of *Kundalini Yoga*, when the *Kundalini* or latent potential life-force in the root or first *chakra* travels unobstructed to the higher centers.

When you practice *pranayama* effectively, the veil of dark ignorance that covers the inner light is removed. *Pranayama* leads to the removal of the obstacles that distract the mind, so that it becomes easy to concentrate and meditate, which will eventually result in enlightenment and self-realization. This has been stated by the great *Rishi Vasistha*, who was the mentor of the divine incarnation, *Rama* in verse 78.46 of the Yoga Vasistha:

> *The wise ones declare that the mind is caused*
> *by the movement of prana*
> *By the practice of pranayama, the mind is stilled.*
> *When the mind ceases its movement,*
> *the world-illusion dissolves [Nirvana]*

The Physical health benefits of Breath Training and Therapy

When you watch an infant sleeping, it is easy to determine that it is breathing primarily by using the diaphragm because you can see the abdomen rise and fall, with each breath. It would stand to reason that teaching chronically ill adults to practice diaphragmatic breathing, rather than habitual chest pattern breathing, could restore their health.

Indeed, researches in China, India and Russia have shown that over 90% of the patients with peptic ulcers can be successfully treated with breathing exercises. Russian research [Kreme Sanatorium] has also have shown successful treatment of tuberculosis patients, while Indian research supports the treatment of patients with hypertension.

Much more research, especially in the United States would be needed to uncover all the potential health benefits of Breath Training and Therapy.

However, we do not need to wait for the results from modern researchers to confirm the insights of thousands of years of yogic science, or what can be confirmed by your own efforts for a few weeks!

Breath and Emotional Release

Have you noticed that when you are depressed, your posture slumps and your breathing becomes constricted? When we are happy, we tend to stand taller and breathe more fully. It appears that our breathing varies with our moods. As you become more aware of your breathing, you will become more aware of your emotional states, and the quality of your thoughts.

Awareness of the emotions does not by itself provide a relief. Noticing your depression or anger does not make them go away. The Complete *Yogic* Breath can be used to help release the negative emotions, and strengthen the positive ones

The process is to first uncover the underlying emotion. Then decide on an antidote – the opposing or healing emotion. Now, with every exhalation, consciously release and expel the negative emotion, while with every inhalation, breath in the positive emotion. The *Yogic* breathing will first bring calm and then a sense of control and eventually joy. Repeat an affirmation which suggests the emotion, such as, "I feel more and more joy [or love etc.]"

However, this breathing release of emotions can only be a short-term healing, unless the underlying behavior that is supporting the negative emotions are modified. This takes deeper awareness, insight, and a high degree of self-discipline, as taught in the practice of meditation.

Where Does The Tortoise Go?

As the tortoise is able to draw in its limbs, so should the yogi draw in his sense organs.
- Gorakshanath

Human beings have three normal states of consciousness, the wakeful state, the dream state and the dreamless sleep state. During the wakeful state, the five sense organs – nose, tongue, eyes, skin and ears are active and continuously sending sense data concerning the five subtle senses of smell, taste, sight, touch and hearing to the mind. It is the mind which classifies, categorizes and censors the sense data under the direction of the ego and generates thoughts and emotions based on the karmic programs encoded at birth and subsequently modified in life.

It is our common experience that the contacts with sensory objects bring only momentary pleasures and are truly the source of pain. As we mature, we perceive that these objects of pleasure have a beginning and an end, and even while enjoying them, we fear losing them or have begun desires for other sensory objects. The fear of loss and desire for more continuously propel us towards our path to doom. Those who are wise will make an effort to stop this cycle of pain.

The sense organs are still sending signals during dream states and dreamless sleep states, but these signals are ignored, unless of some dramatic intensity. There is a partial withdrawal of the sense organs from activity.

When the yogi consciously withdraws from the senses by pulling back the energies normally turned outwards so that they are now turned inwards, then there is the beginning of the fourth state of consciousness, a super-conscious state of awareness. The five gross sense organs are normally turned towards external objects in the wakeful state, and as external objects are sensed, they attach themselves to the mind which consequently becomes agitated.

In the intermediate state of *pratyahara*, or sense-withdrawal, the sense organs are turned inwards under the direction of the mind and become internalized, allowing the mind to subsequently become still. Conversely, if the mind can be stilled, then the sense-organs would no longer be focused outwards. It is difficult to use the will alone to order an agitated mind and command the sense-organs to turn inwards.

In Kriya Yoga, it is by means of the breath that the sense-organs are turned inwards and the mind stilled. The process of *pranayama* (breath and life-force control) assisted by the power of *mantra* (sacred words of power), stills the mind and causes the withdrawal of the sense-organs. This is because when the life-force or *prana* is controlled and stilled, the mind is stilled, and when the mind is stilled, the sense-organs are turned inwards.

Lord Krishna has said:

> *Shutting out all outside contacts, fixing the gaze between the eyebrow, inhaling the exhaling evenly within the nostrils, controlling the senses, the mind and the soul, the wise one devoted to the highest goal of liberation, renouncing desire, fear and anger, achieves the complete liberation.*
>
> Bhagavad Gita 5. 27-28

For the Kriya Yogi, *pratyahara* is not a separate practice, but the continuing or fruit from the practice of *pranayama*. As the *pranayama* process unfolds, sense-withdrawal happens, and the tortoise withdraws its limbs.

There are two levels of sense-withdrawal. In the first, there is detachment from the gross external objects. In this state, the practitioner is no longer disturbed by gross external sensory input. By gross is meant what we normally perceive in the external world with our five sense organs. However, there are subtle sensory objects of which we are not normally aware. In the second phase, there is detachment from the subtle sensory objects and the subtle sense organs are turned inwards.

The key to successful sense-withdrawal is the cultivation of detachment. Until the cessation of mental activity is accomplished, there will be a tendency towards the outward pull of likes and dislikes, of attachment and aversion. Whenever the mind becomes restless, the breath becomes restless and the sense-organs are turned outwards to grasp at external objects.

> *The fickle mind is indeed restless and difficult to control, but by constant practice and detachment from worldly objects, it can be restrained.*
>
> Bhagavad Gita 6.35

The mind is restrained by the cultivation of the five mental constraints or *yamas* which we have previously discussed. The *yamas* are the first *pada* or step of the *ashtanga* yoga and is essential as a foundation for the Kriya Yoga. The practices of the five self-restraints pull energy away from the external world as defined by the ego-centric perspective. They align the practitioner with the internal center or Divine Guiding Principle so that it is possible to become detached from the sensory world.

The essence of *brahmacharya* is the turning inwards of the impulse to seek sensory gratification outwards. Therefore, until complete sense-withdrawal is attained, it is not possible to be a *brahamacharya,* although the effort is made. In the same way, although we start our spiritual life with the *yamas*, their actual perfection cannot be attained until Self-Realization is attained.

The mind-stuff from which arises the mind or *manas*, as well as the ego or *ahamkara* is called *chitta*, and is a subtle matter that comprises the three primary constituents called *gunas* of light, movement and

125

inertia. Normally the mind changes rapidly from one mode to the next, from light to movement to inertia to movement and so on and so forth. Sometimes the mind is mired in inertia and a lot of effort is necessary to use it. Other times, it is like the proverbial monkey flitting from one activity to another and totally unrestrained. By the practice of the five restraints, the *chitta* is purified in the sense that it becomes more of light. Further purification is attained by the entering into sense-withdrawal.

As the process of *pratyahara* continues, it gradually merges into the state of *dharana* or pure concentration, whereby the very thoughts come under control.

Breaking the Barriers to Concentration

The state of pure concentration is called *dharana* and is a natural flowering from *pranayama* or life-force control and *pratyahara* (sense-withdrawal). In Kriya Yoga, it happens during process of intense and prolonged *pranayama*, and does not strictly speaking require separate techniques to develop. However, what many practitioners nowadays forget is that there were stricter qualifications required in the past for initiation into the higher spiritual practices, and the students already prepared with years of basic concentration exercises, self-restraints, and basic breathing techniques, and can also sit in stable posture for hours.

In the absence of adequate preparation, the entering into higher states such as *dharana* is more difficult, and it is in the interest of the sincere student to make some self-effort to cultivate such basic abilities.

Additionally, during the course of the spiritual evolution engendered by Kriya Yoga, barriers to attainment of concentration occur, and one must need to overcome them:

1. appreciating the need for developing concentration:
   Those who take up spirituality may have some pre-conceived notions that they can let go of mental effort. However, just as successful execution in the material world requires a high degree of concentration, so also on the spiritual path. Before the higher "effortless" states are reached, concentrated effort is needed. It is a level of mental self-control for which many exercises have been given by the ancient yogis.
   In the first stage, concentration on some external object such as a figure on the wall helps to develop focus. In the second stage, concentration is on an external part of the body such as the tip of the nose to develop single-pointedness. In the third stage, concentration is on an internal object, such as a mental image of an object to increase internal focus. Finally, in the

fourth stage, concentration on the breath develops internal single-pointedness. This leads to the state of *dharana*, in which the mind is constrained on a single object, but there are still multiple thoughts grouped around the single object. This is the critical difference between dharana and *dhyana* or the meditative absorptive state in which there is only a single thought.

2. Uncontrolled emotionality:
   During the course of the *sadhana* or prescribed spiritual practice, there is a heightened sensitivity to emotions due to the increased awareness of the flow of thoughts. If the *sadhak* or practitioner has not learned to control his emotional reactions, then there can be breakage of concentration. It is only be the continuous practice of detachment from emotions that concentration can be achieved. It does not matter whether the emotions are positive and inspiring or whether they are negative and depressing, all emotions must be controlled and not indulged in during the session.

3. Lack of energy:
   Energy is required to take off on the rocket-ship towards Self-Realization and overcome the gravity of our ignorance. If there is a lack of energy due to overwork in the office or an indulgent life-style, then there will be insufficient energy to provide the momentum to move from *pranayama* to *pratyahara* to *dharana*. It is advisable to review one's life-style choices – whether it is more rewarding to watch less television and devote more time and energy to one's spiritual life or vice-versa. Although Kriya Yoga is meant for the householder who has to earn a living, there is a trade-off between over-work and spiritual practice – is the amount of time spent on work necessary or is there ambition involved? Is there fear of losing one's job involved?

4. Identification with the body:

   The lack of a healthy body is a threat to attaining concentration because we all know that pain takes over and interferes with any effort to focus on anything other than the pain! However, it is not the aches and pains that are the main problem, it is our identification with them – the thought that "I am in pain," rather than that "this body is in pain." The latter thought can be detached from, whereas, the former cannot.

   We have to instill the discipline of understanding that each of us have a body and is a soul with a body, and not a body that happens to have a soul.

   Only when identification with the body is weakened, can there be some form of physical stability. The purpose of the *asanas* to provide for physical stability cannot occur unless there is a simultaneous realization of the role of the body as a physical garment worn by the soul.

5. Identification with the mind and mental fluctuations:

   Even when one can detach from identification with the physical body, there is still a tendency to identify with the mind, to confuse the mind with the soul. Due to this identification with the mind, there is continuous disturbance from mental fluctuations or thoughts. As long as one takes ownership of the thoughts, one cannot attain to the peaceful and calm state of total concentration.

Meditation Happens

The primary cause of bondage as well as of liberation of human beings is the mind. There are two types of minds: pure and impure. A mind having desires is impure and one without desires is a pure mind. A mind full of desires binds while one free of desires liberates. It is therefore necessary for a spiritual aspirant to give up desires of worldly enjoyments in order to attain to the state of meditation.

After withdrawing the mind from the miasma of the sense-organs, the practitioner constraints the mind by focusing the attention on a suitable object of contemplation and concentrating on attaining a single thought. As the state of meditation or *dhyana* happens, nothing else exists in one's consciousness, except the single thought.

It is important that the object of contemplation be one that can be inspiring. If the mind becomes concentrated on a negative thought and that negative thought became the single thought, then there can be terrible consequences. Many stories of the great yogic heroes battling demonic forces or evil humans with fantastic powers show that there have been erring beings that have used the power of meditation for purposes other than for Self-Realization.

The process of meditation follows the achievement of concentration that follows from sense-withdrawal that in turn follows from control of life-force energy. In order for meditation to happen, the mind must be purified from all other thoughts save the one thought that is the focus of the meditation. Since the mind is made up of the three *gunas* or principles of manifestation, it requires that the principle of inertia or *tamas* be absorbed into the principle of *rajas* or activity and restlessness. Next, the principle of rajas has to be absorbed into the principle of light or *sattva*. Then finally, even the principle of *sattva* must be discarded and left behind. The mind is normally an interplay of these *gunas* with one taking the lead and controlling the mind while the other two lie dormant.

> *Through yogic practice, purity is accomplished, as a result of which knowledge is unveiled and true discrimination is gained. Through sattva guna, the detachment of the mind is accomplished and from that state, the Self is realized.*
> Maitri Upanishad IV.3

The following parable is used to shed some light on the *gunas* and the mind:

Once there were three thieves and they would lie in wait at the side of a road to attack travelers. One night, they saw a single man on his horse and attacked him, pulling him off his mount. The poor man struggled but was soon beaten up and bound by them.

They went through his clothes and took all his money. Then the first thief thought to kill the man, but the other two objected. The second thief suggested that they find a ditch and throw him into it so that they would be safe. The third thief agreed and so they threw him into a nearby ditch and left. A little later, the third thief secretly came back and untied the victim. The good thief brought the man out of the ditch and helped him on his way back to the road.

The man was very grateful and wished to thank the thief for his kindness. He was a very rich man and offered to take the thief home with him. The thief smiled and shook his head. He told the man that he meant no harm but due to circumstances had become a thief and that it was his nature. It would not be possible for him to go with the man to his home.

The first thief is the ignorance or *tamas guna* while the second is restlessness or *rajas guna*. The third thief is *sattva guna* and even though the light of intelligence shines from it, it is responsible for manifestation.

Many obstacles arise during the process of mind purification. The deadliest obstacle is that of illusions. A seeker often fails to correctly evaluate the level of his progress and through over-enthusiasm promotes ego-inflation. When obstructions or reality sets in so does disillusionment leading to depression and the giving up of effort.

The yogic path has many steps that can generate illusions making the seeker "high" at one time and "low" at another time. A sincere seeker has to give up such worries and doubts as well as thoughts of self-aggrandisement.

Perseverance is the key to attainment. The illusive thoughts are a type of *vrittis* or modification of consciousness and are caused by inadequate or incomplete experiences. A competent guide is very necessary at times of crisis, to sort out the untruth from the truth and the important from the unimportant. The seeker has to continue practice with patience and faith to overcome all obstacles.

Amazing Grace

Not long after a spiritual seeker embarks on the path towards the Divine, he or she will be encountering the concept and reality of grace or *kripa*. This is so whether one follows a devotional, intellectual, specialized or integrated path; whether it is God's grace or Guru's grace, it will be made abundantly clear that without this ingredient in the mix, success in or completion of the path is not possible.

The traditional view of grace has always bothered me because it didn't make much sense to me that the Divine or the Guru as Divine surrogate would arbitrarily choose someone to bestow his grace on whether that person deserved it or not. In fact, there are stories where no rhyme nor reason can be established for this arbitrariness.

Just as there are physical laws, there are spiritual laws established during creation. An important law is that of Karma, which has been dealt with in more detail elsewhere in this volume. This law is one of causation by which every action has an appropriate reaction. As it is said in all ancient scriptures - you reap what you sow. The *yogis* say that our current actions, thoughts and words determine our future state. Why would the Divine suddenly decide to over-rule the law of Karma? Some would say why not, since the Divine can do anything.

There are generally three ways to approach the concept of grace:

1. Its all a matter of grace, and self effort is irrelevant:

> *God is not revealed by delivering or hearing sermons or developing sharp intellect. Whosoever God chooses, to him is He revealed. One who obtains the grace of God, to him God reveals Himself in reality.*
>
> Katha Upanishad

This is the least satisfying in that there is no scope for personal effort, since no matter what actions are taken, they cannot lead to reality. There is a gap between human effort and reality which can only be filled by grace. No rationale can be given for why some get it and others do not.

2. One has to do one's best and then one needs to leave the actual results to Divine grace:

    > *Dedicate all your actions to Me; you will obtain My grace.*
    > Lord Krishna in the Bhagavad Gita

    There is intense effort needed to get Divine grace. The following activities are generally cited as necessary but not sufficient for attracting grace:

    - Study of scriptures
    - Practice of Yoga and meditation
    - Austerities such as fasting, silence and intense praying
    - Satsangs or meeting with saints and sages
    - Pilgrimages to sacred spots

3. It's all our own effort and grace is the operation of the positive *karma* from past lives:
    This is the most satisfying from the rational perspective, since it gives the highest priority to our own activities. It is well-established that our future is governed by our present activities and our present has been conditioned by our past. When we do positive actions such as those pointed out in the last section, we accumulate the karma that can generate positive results in this life under the right circumstances. We call this grace because we cannot link the present result with the past cause. This doesn't mean that the linkage doesn't exist.

if one considers carefully the second and third alternatives, there is not much difference. In both cases, the spiritual seeker has to perform certain prescribes activities in order to obtain grace. The only difference is that in one case grace is a special dispensation earned by the seeker and in the second case, grace is merely another name for past good *karma*, and has no separate existence. In either case, proper action is required. In the first case, it appears that there is no need for any action, since all action is futile. This is the purely devotional mode of apprehension and can lead to religious apathy. From a *yogic* perspective, since our suffering has been compounded by our own actions, it is necessary that we make our best effort to rectify the situation.

The sages have counseled that even *yogis* must invoke the grace of the Divine in order to achieve liberation and so we cannot blindly sit and wait for a capricious intervention nor egotistically think that the Divine has no role to play in our redemption. A middle path is usually appropriate and practical.

> *The Divine is hiding in the cave of the sacred heart*
> *of every being as the Universal Self (Paramatma).*
> *That soul becomes free from all misery when it sees*
> *the glory of God by His grace.*
> Shveteshvatara Upanishad

Devotion

Bhakti is the practice as well as the state of spiritual devotion to the Divine. It is not an ephemeral emotional state, but a constant turning of one's energies towards the Divine. It is the most popular and yet most misunderstood form of spiritual practice.

According to the *Bhakti Sutras*, a pre-eminent text on this practice:

> *Spiritual devotion is developed by relinquishing objects and relinquishing attachments.*
> Bhakti Sutras 35

There is no room for attachments to any objects or desires – there is only the fullness of Divine in one's life. For there to be devotion to the Lord, one must develop the purity of the *yamas,* leading to contentment and equanimity.

Further insight is given about devotion, in *sutra* 7, 8,9,10, where it is stated:

> *Spiritual devotion does not arise from desire. Its nature is a state of inner stillness.*
>
> *This inner stillness consecrates the performance of worldly and traditional social duties.*
>
> *Inner stillness furthermore requires a single-hearted intention and disinterest in what is antagonistic to spiritual devotion.*
>
> *When one is single-hearted, one relinquishes seeking security in anything other than the Divine.*

In Tulsidasa's retelling of the epic Ramayana, there is an episode in which prince Rama meets with a lady saint who asks him for instruction on how to practice devotion. The divine incarnation of the Lord instructed her by giving a nine-fold way to devotion.

1. associate with saintly people
2. Enjoy stories of divinity and divinely inspired beings
3. perform selfless service as an expression of love
4. sing of the divine qualities or characteristics without any selfish motivation
5. recite mantras with full faith, the path illuminated by the Vedas
6. Perform all actions with tranquility and to see all circumstances as opportunities to manifest perfection
7. See the world as equal to God and to regard the company of saintly beings as even a greater opportunity than the perception of God
8. Be satisfied with whatever one receives as the fruit of one's actions and not to contemplate the fault of others
9. To remain with simplicity all the time, renouncing devious planning for selfish ends and to take delight in faith in God with neither high nor low emotions.

A being that practices even one of these steps of devotion is beloved of God.

However, it is critical to remember that no matter how great one's efforts are, they are not sufficient of themselves to develop the true essence of *bhakti*. It is only by the grace of the Divine, that spiritual devotion is fully manifested:

> *But spiritual devotion is primarily developed from the grace of the Divine via the blessing of a great Soul.*
> Bhakti Sutras 38

There is a great variety among human beings, and due to *karmic* tendencies, spiritual devotion can be developed according to five different attitudes towards the Divine:

- As a servant of the Divine
- As a friend of the Divine
- As a child of the Divine
- As a disciple of the Divine
- As a spouse of the Divine

All five attitudes towards the Divine have their unique aspects, as far as spiritual relationships are concerned, and cannot be judged or rated as better or worse. It would take a separate book to even begin to do justice to the whole subject of spiritual devotion, and all we can do is give a framework for further development.

Traditionally, there are said to be four levels of consciousness in spiritual devotion, and some may say that they are given in order of progressively higher dimensions:

- Worshipful state of consciousness
- Prayerful state of consciousness
- Meditative state of consciousness
- Unified state of consciousness

Until one is fully merged with the Divine, it is always possible to return to a state of confusion and ignorance, and so there is an injunction to continue one's practice even after the development of spiritual devotion:

> *Let there be a firm commitment to maintaining an ethical code, even after the development of spiritual devotion. Otherwise, there is the risk of a fall.*
> Bhakti Sutras 12,13

Once there was a king who was a great devotee of Lord Shiva and he had built a great temple to the Divine and was awaiting the auspicious day and time for the inaugural ceremonies. He had spent years and great wealth in the planning, architecture and building of the temple and was really pleased with the result.

At the same time, in a nearby village a *yogi* who only had a single loincloth and a begging bowl went about and asked the villagers to help him build a temple to the Lord. However, they rejected him because they felt that he was only a poor beggar who could never manage to build a temple. The yogi felt sorry for the villagers and went down to the bank of a river and sat down under a tree. He meditated and said to the Lord, "I want to express my devotion to you and demonstrate my love by building a temple that will benefit the people, but nobody will help me.

The *yogi* went deeper into meditation and selected the piece of vacant land for the temple. He then purified the land with a great fire ceremony. With utmost devotion he chanted the Lord's mantra one hundred thousand times. Then he made the foundation with bricks on which he had inscribed Shiva's name, while reciting His praises. In his mind, the temple was taking shape and form and had high walls and a roof on top which rested His trident. Finally, the *yogi* installed the Shiva-lingam in the holy of holies, and meditated on His eternal presence.

That very night, Lord Shiva appeared in the king's dream and asked him to postpone the inauguration ceremony. The king was shaken and argued that all the preparation had been made, with thousands of participants already in the city. However, the Lord said, "I'm busy tomorrow and will not be coming."

The king asked what could be more important and the Lord told him that he was going to so-and-so village for the installation of another temple.

When the king awoke, he sent for his ministers and priests and told them to cancel the ceremony, and get his retinue ready for a trip to the nearby village. He ignored their protestations. As he reached the village, he ordered the elders to appear before him and questioned them about their temple. They were surprised and denied any such building's existence. But the king knew he could not be mistaken and so asked them if anyone had planned to build a temple. They nervously mentioned the crazy *yogi* who had been meditating near the river.

When the king and his retinue and the whole village went down to the river, they beheld a great temple made of the finish stones and the yogi was be blessed by the presence of the Great Lord Himself. Such was the power of his devotion.

Dispassion

Vairagya or dispassion is detachment from worldly objects and ultimately from the three principles of existence, the *gunas*. It is our desires and aversions that force us into relationships with objects. We need to recognize that these desires do not reflect our true needs. The desires arise from our false conception of reality, of the self rather than the Self, and its illusive relationship with objects.

All spiritual practitioners must cultivate and perfect dispassion. Yoga is not achieved by the techniques alone. Patanjali in his Yoga Sutras (1.2) has revealed that, "Yoga is the restriction of the fluctuations of consciousness." The modifications of consciousness are the cause of our normal non-realized state and when these fluctuations no longer afflict the consciousness, there is freedom from desires and the consequent suffering.

Further, the great *yogi* has given the recipe for Yoga in 1.12: "The restriction of the fluctuations is achieved through practice and dispassion." Therefore, *vairagya* is necessary and has to be cultivated together with one's *sadhana* or spiritual practice.

There are various methods traditionally used for achieving dispassion. These include:
- Intellectual analysis to dispel the false conception of reality
- Creating a strong desire into which all other desires are subsumed. This is generally achieved by recognition that the only true desire is the desire for God
- Expanding selfish desires into Universal Love

Dispassion can also arise from the repeated experience of *samadhi* (super-conscious state of bliss) or by a vision of the True Self.

The analysis of desires will lead to a realization that a desire does not equate to a true need. Desires come and go and what seemed very important last week may now seem unnecessary. A desire does not have an absolute value – we can entertain multiple desires at any moment, some are stronger and some are weaker. Desires are impermanent because they are related to objects and all objects are impermanent.

It takes great effort to satisfy our desires by acquiring objects. There is greater effort expanded to keep and guard them, and finally, one is consumed with regret when one loses them. At any moment, we are beset by multiple desires jostling for our attention and eventually, one of them takes the lead and demands satisfaction. One makes the appropriate effort to satisfy this desire and there is temporary satisfaction and fleeting happiness, followed by another desire coming to the foreground. The new desire leads to a temporary disillusionment with the hard-earned attainment of the previous one, followed by the thought that maybe the new one will give true satisfaction.

In this way, if one can give up one's illusions and see through the disappointments, one can release all the energy locked up with preserving the illusions.

The process is continuous until by the power of *samadhi*, even the latent desires in the causal body rises up and can be seen and removed. These desires are dormant and do not normally show themselves, but may when given the right circumstances. A rich person may be honest because he has been taught to be so and has never had any reason to be otherwise. However, only when he loses his money, will he discover whether he is truly honest or only suppressing dishonesty.

Let us consider the following parable to help us be free from the bondage of desires:

A young *sadhu* who had devoted himself to the practice of yoga was visiting a temple and encountered the daughter of a rich merchant. She talked to him for some time about his life and the places he'd been.

They fell instantly in love with each other, or at least so believed themselves to be. The desire to be with her was overwhelming and he considered giving up his spiritual practice and returning to the householder ways. She told him where she was staying and asked him to see her next day, as she would be leaving with her father on the journey to return home in a distant part of the country.

In the night the *sadhu* prayed at the image of Lord Shiva. He prayed to be free of his temptation. However, the desire grew stronger. He started to repeat the Lord's mantra but his mind was clouded. He fell asleep and when morning came, he made up his mind to join the merchant and win his daughter's hand in marriage.

He became an apprentice in the merchant's business and then over time became his most trusted assistant because of his hard work and sharp mind. He then asked for the daughter's hand in marriage and soon had a family and took over the business after the merchant's passing away.

He was happy and contented. Then fate took a turn and he lost his whole family to a plague. Soon after, in his grief, he began to take interest in the welfare of others, participating in charities. However, due to his neglect, the business suffered and he lost everything to his unscrupulous partners.

As a beggar he wandered around the pilgrimage sites wondering what his life had been about. He became totally disillusioned and began to teach others about the futility of desires.

One night, the broken old man wandered into a temple and sat in front of the Lord's image. He then discovered that it was the same temple from which he had abandoned his spiritual life. He prayed for forgiveness and fell asleep with tears in his eyes.

Next morning he awoke and was astonished to discover that he was still a young sadhu and that it had all been a dream. He had lost all desire for the girl and married life. With renewed vigor he pursued this spiritual path and soon achieved liberation.

The first step towards dispassion is to identify the source and nature of desires and achieve freedom from them.

Samadhi

Samadhi happens only –
when mind disappears.
Why ask what happens?
What a joke!
Those who know speak not
Those who speak, know not

Samadhi happens only –
when mind disappears.
Beware the mind's cheap tricks,
snakes from sticks!
Sages compassionate words twisted.
Ego-mind false visions created.

Samadhi happens only –
when mind disappears.
Like tortoise body-sense still,
by concentrated breath, let mind still.
From the many to one to none.
From still mind to no-mind to self-effulgent Sun.

Part 3

The Light that Shines

Dharma

It is not enough that the spiritual practitioner is purified by the practice of self-restraint. The eradication of the *karmic* storehouse or *sanchita karma* requires perfection in *dharma*.

The word *dharma* is from *dhri* – to sustain, carry, hold – that which contains or upholds the cosmos. It is a complex, all-inclusive term with many meanings, including: divine law, law of being, way of righteousness, religion, duty, responsibility, virtue, justice, goodness and truth.

Essentially, *dharma* is the orderly fulfillment of an inherent nature or destiny – each of us has his or her *dharma* – the best path to self-realization. Relating to the soul, it is the mode of conduct most conducive to spiritual advancement, the right and righteous path.

There are four principal kinds of *dharma*:

- *Rita* : universal law - the inherent order of the universe. The law of being and nature that contain and govern all forms, functions and processes, from galaxy clusters to the power of mental thought and perception. This is also the foundation of all physical and scientific laws.

- *Varna dharma*: social duty – law of one's own kind. This defines an individual's obligations and responsibilities within the nation, society, community, class, occupational subgroup and family. An important part of this *dharma* is religious moral law.

- *Asrama dharma*: duties of life's stages. Human *dharma*. The natural process of maturing from childhood to old age through fulfillment of the duties of each of the four stages of life –

147

brahmachari (student), *grihasta* (householder), *vanaprastha* (elder advisor), and *sannyasa* (religious recluse) – in pursuit of the four human goal : *dharma* (righteousness), *artha* (wealth), *kama* (pleasure) and *moksha* (liberation).

- *Svadharma*: personal law – one's perfect individual pattern through life, according to one's own particular physical, mental and emotional nature. *Svadharma* is determined by the sum of past *karma*s and the cumulative effect of the other three *dharma*s. It is the individualized application of *dharma*, dependent on personal *karma*, reflected on one's race, community, physical characteristics, health, intelligence, skills and aptitudes, desires and tendencies, religion, *sampradaya* [spiritual lineage], family and *guru*.

A part of the social duty of each person is called the principle of good conduct that is applicable to all people regardless of age, gender or class. It is listed in the ancient *Manu Sastras* as : steadfastness, forgiveness, self-restraint, non-stealing, cleanliness, sense control, high-mindedness, learning, truthfulness, absence of anger. These are also called *samanya dharma* – the general duty of all beings.

The sages of old were wise enough to provide for exceptions to the general rules, and called it *apad dharma* or emergency conduct, for which the only rigid rule is wisdom. Exceptional situations may require deviating from normal rules of conduct, with the condition that such exceptions are to be made only for the sakes of others, not for personal advantage.

Thoughts, words or deeds that transgress divine law in any of the human expressions of *dharma* is unrighteousness and is called *adharma*. They bring the accumulation of demerits called *papa*, while *dharma* brings merit, called *punya*.

It is by the practice of *niyama* or the self discipline of observances that the spiritual seeker is transformed into a perfected being who is the essence of *dharma*.

Through active practice [*tapas*] and self-study [*svadyaya*], the *yogi* becomes united with *dharma*. It is said that if one knows and acts according to one's dharma, then one is pure [*saucha*], content [*santosha*], and surrendered to the divine will [*ishvar pranidhana*].

It is well to remember the ancient prescription to do what one is meant to be: "better one's *svadharma* even imperfectly performed that the *dharma* of another well-performed." By performing the duty prescribed by one's own nature (*svabhava*) one incurs no demerits or bad *karma*. This is not a recipe for apathy or be satisfied with one's mediocrity – it is an active search of one's highest potential. It is not a recipe for justifying an unjust caste system based on birth – it is an active movement to higher levels regardless of circumstances. However, it is better to be a happy and superb baker than to be forced into being an unhappy and mediocre doctor.

The following two parables deal with dharma. The first one is especially difficult for contemporary readers to understand or accept. The concept of doing one's duty, even one as ephemeral as being the host of an undesired guest, to such lengths seem very alien to our society. The whole concept of sacrificing oneself for the sake of dharma requires a mind set where the body is not identified as the Self.

The second parable deals with the situation that happens when two persons have opposing duties. What happens and how can this be resolved?

Parable 3: Dharma and Sacrifice

Once upon a time there was a hunter who lurked in a forest looking out for birds that he might trap with his nets. He had a wicked nature, being steeped in ignorance and his countenance reflected his dark nature. He had bloodshot eyes and looked like a henchman of Death. His legs were long and his feet were short. His mouth was large and his cheek bulged out. He had no friend or kinsman. Everybody kept away from him disgusted with his evil ways.

He used to earn his living by catching birds in a net he spread out in the forest and selling their meat. In this way, he lived for many years untroubled by any consciousness of his sinful conduct, for he killed more than was necessary for feeding himself. Long habit had blunted the edge of his conscience and dulled his sense of a virtuous life.

On a particular day, as he was wandering in the woods in quest of birds, there rose a great storm and lightning leaped from side to side. The sky was overcast with dark clouds and then it poured heavily and in a moment, water was everywhere.

The hunter was filled with unspeakable dread. Shivering with cold and trembling with fear, he roamed listlessly through the forest. In vain he looked about for a dry spot. Every path and every eminence was under water.

Many a bird fell down dead blasted by the wind and rain. The wild animals roamed about alone or in packs filled with fear and looking out for a shelter.

Through the storm, he saw a female pigeon on the ground stiff with cold. Despite his own problems, used to evil habits, he picked up the distressed bird and put her in his cage.

Just then, he saw close by a tree taller than the rest, to which many birds had flocked to for refuge from the fury of the weather. It stood there in its lordly height like a good man intent on giving aid to those in affliction.

Soon, the sky cleared and he could see the blue sky studded with stars. The wicked hunter turned his steps homeward still shivering with cold. He saw that it was late and his home was a long way off, and so, he decided to spend the night under the tall tree. Making a bed of the leaves that lay strewn about, he stretched out to sleep resting his head on a stone.

It so happened that there was a male pigeon that had made his nest on a branch of that tree. This pigeon was in intense anguish that his mate who had earlier gone out in quest of food had not returned though it was already dark. "It has been a terrible storm," he cried, "and my dear wife has not yet come back. What could have happened to her? Is she free from any harm? I already miss her."

It is said in the scriptures that though filled with sons and grandsons, daughters and daughters-in-law, with servants and others, a householder's home is still empty if there is no wife. The house by itself does not deserve that name. It is the wife that makes the home. A house without a wife is truly a wilderness.

The pigeon further lamented, "If my wife of eyes ruby red, of bright plumage and sweet voice does not return, what use is my life to me? Constant in her duty, she would not eat if I have not eaten; she would not bathe till I have bathed. She would not sit before I have sat down or lie down to sleep till I go to bed."

"Sharing my joys and sorrows, she would feel forlorn when I am away and she would turn my wrath by her gentle speech. Devoted to me, her lord, and resigning herself to me, she used to be ever intent on my welfare. Fortunate is he who has a wife like mine. One can revel in the joys of a sweet home with such a wife though living at the foot of a tree. Without her, life even in a palace will be dark and dreary."

"The wife is a true helpmate in the pursuit of the goals of life such as truth or *dharma*, wealth or *artha* and pleasures or *kama*. She is the trusted friend when one travels away from home. A man comes alone into the world and leaves it alone. During his sojourn in it, his wife keeps him faithful company."

"In disease and distress, there is no friend like a wife; there is none like her who can give a man solace and comfort. There is none so dear like the wife, no refuge like her in the world. And in doing acts of *dharma*, none can stand by a person and help him so dutifully like his wife."

The she-pigeon who had been caught in a cage by the hunter was the very wife of the pigeon crying out and when she heard these lamentations of her lord, she said to herself, "How fortunate am I that my lord speaks so highly of me whatever be my nature, good or bad! She is no wife whose husband is not pleased with her. If a woman's husband is satisfied, then that gives satisfaction to all her gods."

Reflecting like this, despite her affliction in the hunter's cage, the she-pigeon spoke to her woe-stricken mate: "Listen, my lord," said she, "to my words and act on them to obtain merit. It is your opportunity to rescue your inadvertent guest, for here is this hunter who sleeps at your door. His limbs are stiff with cold and he is tired and hungry. Show him your hospitality, for it is said in the scriptures that, to let a supplicant die of cold and hunger at your door is a sin as heinous as killing a pure good man or a cow which feeds the world."

"It is clear that our *dharma* is to help this poor man and you know it. So, stand by it. We have heard that he who performs his appointed *dharma* to the extent of his powers goes after death to regions of supreme bliss."

"You have sons and daughters and there is nothing else of earthly goods for you to secure in this life. So give up attachment to your body.

Offer what is due to this huner so that his heart may be pleased. In that way, you will earn merit and your life will be truly purposeful."

The male pigeon had tears of joy flowing from his eyes, for he had heard what his mate had said and was pleased with her wise and *dharmic* words. Immediately, he resolved to honor the dreadful hunter and show him every hospitality.

Addressing the bird-slayer in terms of due humility, the bird said: "Welcome, guest, welcome this day to my abode. I shall wait on you. Tell me what you will have me do. Do not grieve or stand on any ceremony. This is your home. Tell me quickly, what I may do for you; what is your desire? You have sought refuge under me and so you are dear and sacred to me."

For it is said, "Even an enemy must be received with hospitality when he comes to a person's house. The tree does not withdraw its shade from him who comes to cut it. He cannot live happily in this world nor attain salvation in the next who fails in the duties of hospitality."

Hearing these words of the bird, the hunter replied; "Protect me from this cold which freezes my limbs."

The pigeon happily carried a small dry twig to a place where there was a fire, lit the twig with it and carried it back to the foot of the tree. Collecting the dry leaves, he set fire to them and made a big fire.

"Warm yourself in this fire without fear from any quarter," the bird chirped to the hunter.

Warmed and refreshed, he spoke to his winged host and asked for food to appease his hunger.

The bird replied: "Alas! I have not stored anything which I may give you to eat. Like the ascetics of the forest we live day to day without keeping anything for the morrow."

And yet, the bird felt sad and was sad that it was unable to appease the man's hunger.

Soon rousing himself from his melancholy, he told the man: "Wait just for a while for I shall satisfy you." Kindling the fire into a bigger blaze, with joy beaming through his eyes, he exclaimed: "I have heard it from the saints, sages and gods that honoring a guest is a most meritorious act. Please accept my offering."

Steadfast in its resolve and with a joyful face, the bird went thrice round the fire and fell into it intending that the hunter might eat its cooked flesh.

The hunter saw what the bird did, and stood amazed. "What is this that I have done?' he pondered. "Greatly have I sinned and invited dire reproof." And he felt very guilty indeed.

His long suppressed conscience now reared itself. Reproaching himself, he said: "My mind has been wicked and I have committed a heinous sin. This noble bird has taught me a great lesson. He sacrificed his life at the altar of *dharma*."

He further resolved, "From now on, I shall abandon everything, Profiting by the example of this bird, I shall renounce all pleasures. I shall bear hunger and thirst and endure the scorching rays of the sun. I shall starve my flesh through fasts and feed my spirit by penances to make myself eligible for higher worlds."

"Hereafter I shall pursue the path of *dharma*; for dharma is the way and the goal. I shall follow the lead of the pigeon and practice *dharma* even as he has done.'

The hunter threw away his staff, his iron-hook, his net and the cage. He released the she-pigeon from the cage and went forth to roam about in the world and determined not to turn back from his high resolve.

After he left the spot, the she-pigeon, who had been set at liberty, thought of her lord and husband and cried out disconsolately in the extremity of her grief:

"I do not remember even one occasion, my dear lord, she wailed, 'when you have been unkind to me. Miserable is the lot of a widow though she is mother of many sons. You have ever cherished me with love and affection and have always held me in great esteem. We loved one another as we sported together on hill and dale, in the springs of rivers and on tops of trees. We used to soar together in the sky in gentle companionship. Alas! Those joys are gone now!"

"There is no protector to a woman as her husband. Where can she find happiness except in her husband? Even abandoning everything else, she should find refuge in him. What is my life worth when thou art gone? Would a noble wife wish to live after her husband is dead?"

Lamenting like this, she plunged into the blazing fire and immolated herself in its flames.

As her soul was set free of its mortal frame, she beheld her lord shining in ethereal splendor, riding on a celestial car, adored by noble personages. She joined her husband on the chariot and they both ascended to Heaven.

The former hunter saw all this from a distance and he said to himself; "I too shall strive to attain this state by my austerities." He went forward with no thought of food or shelter. He gave up all earthly ties. As he wandered on, he saw a beautiful lake full of colorful lotuses and lovely water-fowl. Though he felt acute thirst and intense weariness, he controlled his mind and desisted from satisfying his thirst or bathing his limbs in the inviting waters.

He penetrated into an adjoining forest infested by beasts of prey. Lacerated and torn by thorns and bleeding all over, he went on and on unmindful of whatever happened to him. Not far off he saw a blazing fire which enveloped the entire forest and consumed everything in its dreadful course.

The reformed hunter ran towards the devouring conflagration. He plunged headlong into it. It turned his frame into ashes and with it burnt away all his sins and purified his soul. And then he found himself in Heaven as well.

Such is the power of *dharma* and sacrifice.

Parable 4: Dueling Dharma

Once there was a great king called Avikshit who ruled over his kingdom for a long time and he was a just king. When he grew old, he entrusted his kingdom to his son Marutta and went himself to the forest with his wife to lead the life of a hermit seeking liberation.

Marutta was an able ruler like his father, never deviating from the path of *dharma* and ever mindful of the welfare of his subjects. He was bold and courageous, skilled in the use of every weapon. True to the obligations of royalty, he performed various fire sacrifices and freely gave away enormous wealth as offerings to the Divine. His subjects were mightily pleased by his bounties and they themselves were constant in the observance of the duties relating to their roles in life.

And thus all was well in every part of the king's domains till, one day, his grandmother who was leading the life of an recluse in the forest sent him news of a great calamity that had befallen the *yogis* doing meditating in the forest.

In her message, the grand old lady admonished: "Your grandsire went to Heaven after ruling his kingdom, earning great merit. Your father has gone to the forest to lead a spiritual life. I am here doing penance. But what is this that I learn that brings ill-repute to you? This is not how your grandsire and your own father conducted the affairs of State. You seem to have lost yourself in sensual pleasures. Do not your informants report to you what happens in the four corners of your kingdom? Else, how can you be unaware of the iniquities perpetrated in your land? Now, listen if you do not know it yourself. The *nagas* or serpents of the nether regions have come out of their hide-outs and plunged their fatal fangs into seven boys who now lie dead; they were sons of the yogis. Not only that. These dreadful serpents have wrought havoc in the sacrificial grounds and polluting them. I do not know if they did all this because these *nagas* have not been propitiated for long by food and prayer proper to them. But, whatever it was, it is a most unrighteous act that these have been guilty of, killing innocent and unoffending children. These yogis themselves could have burnt the serpents to ashes by the power of their *tapas* (inner fire) but they feel that punishment of the wrongdoer is not their office and that it is the duty the king to do it. Remember this, my child: He who is born to be a king can indulge in pleasures only till a crown settles on his head. The moment the waters of his anointment into royalty are poured over him, then begin his cares and anxieties."

"Now that you are king, you must be all eyes and ears. You must be able to distinguish between friends and foes. You must choose your ministers with care and you must be watchful for ever to make sure of the loyalty of those about you. You must gather news of your people as to who among them are intent on *dharma* and who are not. You must find out who deserve to be punished and stretch your arm unflinchingly at them. You must find out who needs protection and take them under your care. Your informants must be very vigilant to gather news from every quarter and you must set others to check on them as well. Thus devoted to the offices of your State, you must remember that the instrument of your body is not for seeking pleasure, but to strive hard, day and night, to discharge your duties properly."

"Therefore, my child, who is now king of this land, abandon the quest for pleasure. Subject yourself to every hardship to rule your kingdom with absolute regard for righteousness. Kept in ignorance of what has happened, you are not aware of the sad plight of these *yogis*. Yours is now the duty to punish the *nagas* who have fatally bitten their children. It is your *dharma* to protect the good and punish the wicked. Else, all the sins of the wicked people will be on your head. I have spoken now; do as you please."

The king heard this message from his grandmother and was aroused by the accusation that he had failed in his duties. He felt extremely angry with himself. He went at once to the hermitage of that worshipful lady and fell at her feet. She blessed him most heartily.

Then, Marutta beheld the seven children lying dead on the ground and he was very distressed at that sight. Straightening himself with indignation, he said: 'Now, let all the worlds peopled with men, gods and demons witness how I shall punish these *nagas* for the heinous crime that they have committed."

So saying, he lifted his mighty bow and yoked it with fire missiles for the destruction of every serpent inhabiting the regions below. Then there arose a mighty fire which enveloped every part of the land of *nagas* and nothing could contain it. The *nagas* ran for their lives here, there and everywhere, crying aloud to father, mother and child to escape the dread terror. The tails of some of them were aflame while the hoods of others were caught in the conflagration, and, in desperate confusion, giving up their ornaments and their apparel, all of them issued out of the nether world and sought refuge at the hands of Marutta's mother. For, once upon a time, she had given them promise of help in times of distress.

Going to her, filled with fear, the *nagas* fell at her feet. In voices choked with agony, they reminded her of her promise of protection and said: "Now has the hour come, great mother, to redeem your promise. Pray give us our lives and order your son to stay his hand"

Marutta's mother in turn implored Avikshit to stop their son, but he replied: "Our son is furious that these *nagas* have been guilty of a great sin. I am afraid he cannot be turned from his resolve."

Still, the *nagas* continued their entreaties: "We fall at your feet and pray for protection. Be merciful to us. It is the duty of a warrior to carry a bow and arrows to save others in distress; is that not so?"

Avikshit heard what the *nagas* said. Agreeing to his wife's desire, he told her: "Well, my dear, this instant I shall go to our son for the protection of the *nagas*. It is true that those who have sought refuge should not be abandoned. If he does not pay heed to my words and persists in his purpose, I shall oppose his fire arrows with mine and prevent him from killing the serpent people."

Taking up his bow and accompanied by his wife, Avikshit went to meet his son. The King saw his father wielding his mighty bow and the terrific arrows waiting for his command to spread universal-destruction.

Avikshit spoke to his son and bade him restrain his anger and withdraw his destructive missiles from the bow.

Marutta looked at his father and again saw him displaying his bow and arrows as if ready to give battle. Bowing to him humbly, he replied: "While I am kind, unmindful of my authority, these serpents have killed the seven children of the *yogis*. They have polluted the waters and ruined the sacrificial altars. They have committed an unpardonable sin for which they deserve to be punished. Do not prevent me from punishing them, my dear father. If I do not punish them, I shall go to hell for failing in my duty."

"Alas, my son! These serpent people have sought my protection. So, for my sake, out of respect for me, withdraw your arrows. Enough of your anger."

"No, dear Father, I shall not forgive these evil-doers who have sinned greatly. How can I agree to what you say? To do as you command me will be to violate my *dharma*. Is it not the duty of a king to visit the wicked with punishment and protect the good? So doing, he goes to holy regions after death. Otherwise, he goes to hell."

Marutta was firm in his resolve and refused to yield though his father and mother pleaded with him most earnestly. Seeing that he would not withdraw his missiles from their death-dealing flight, Avikshit got angry and said: "You are bent on killing these terrified *nagas* who have sought refuge in me. You would not heed to my request. Then, take up my challenge. You are not the only bowman on this earth. I too have missiles not inferior to yours. Stand up and show your valor." With this he fitted a terrible missile to his bow.

As the two missiles of the father and son were poised against each other prepared for deadly combat and threatened the whole land with complete destruction.

Marutta beheld his father's terrible aspect, his fingers toying with the missile which would spell instant death. Facing him, the king asked: "Protection of my subjects is the duty prescribed for me. Would you kill me for performing my dharma?"

However, Avikshit responded: "But protection of those who seek refuge in me is my duty. How can I let you live when you are bent on preventing me from doing my *dharma*? Either you kill me in this combat and then kill these *nagas* as you please; or vanquishing you, I save these *nagas* from death at your hands. It is unrighteous of him who for any reason fails to go to the rescue of those who ask for help, even though they come from the camp of his enemies. I am a warrior and these serpent people are in distress and appeal to me for help. I have promised to save them. How then can I refrain from slaying you if they must be protected?"

Marutta retorted: "Be it friend or kinsman, father or teacher, if a person comes in the king's way of protecting his subjects, such a person deserves to be killed without compunction. Therefore, my father, I must fight against you. Pray do not be angry with me, I must stand up for my *dharma* and if I oppose you, it is not out of anger with you.'

So, they stood against each other, father and son, each one intent on killing the other. The sages of the forest had gathered there in awful suspense of the issue of this strange combat. They told the son not to send his arrow against his father and they appealed likewise to the father to spare his son.

Marutta put them off by saying: "My *dharma* tells me that I should destroy the evil-doers and protect the good. Is that not the duty of a king? Tell me, holy ones, is that wrong?"

Avikshit asked: "Is it not the *dharma* of a person to save one to whom aid in distress has been promised? Is it not a crime to look on while one who has sought refuge is being killed?"

The *yogis* told the father and son: 'But listen, both of you, to what these *nagas* have to say." And the *nagas* said: "We shall restore to life the children bitten by some of our tribe."

Accordingly, they sucked back the poison from the bodies of the victims and the children stood up as before.

Marutta then fell at his father's feet in devout supplication. Avikshit embraced his son fondly and blessed him saying: "Long may you rule over your kingdom; and may you see sons and grandsons and live happily for many, many years!"

It is noteworthy to see that divine intervention is the only resolution to such a sticky situation. No logic can prevail nor mediation.

Karma

Karma is the spiritual law that provides the mechanism which impels the soul to re-incarnate and determines the condition, pre-disposition, genetic code etc. of the new birth, based on the actions of the present and past births.

Karma is one of the most important principles in the *Sanatana dharma*, or ever-present spiritual science of India. The word *karma* has numerous meanings, among them:

- any act or deed
- the principle of cause and effect
- a consequence or "fruit of action" – *Karmaphala* [fruit of action] or *uttarphala* [after effect], which sooner or later returns upon the doer. What we sow, we shall reap in this or future lives. Selfish, hateful acts will bring suffering. Benevolent actions will bring loving reactions.

Karma is a neutral, self-perpetuating law of the inner cosmos, much as gravity is an impersonal law of the outer cosmos. In fact, it has been said that gravity is a small, external expression of the greater law of *Karma*.

The law of *Karma* acts impersonally, yet we may meaningfully interpret its results as either positive [*punya*] or negative [*papa*] – terms describing actions leading the soul either toward or away from the spiritual goal. A good, kind or helpful action increases the store of *punya*, while a harmful action increases one's store of *papa*.

Karma as the fruit of action is threefold: *sanchita, parabdha,* and *kriyamana*:

- *Sanchita Karma*: this is the accumulated fruit of all one's actions – the sum of all *Karma*s of this life and past lives
- *Parabda Karma*: those fruit of actions begun; set in motion. That portion of *sanchita Karma* that is bearing fruit and shaping

the events and conditions of the current life, including the nature of one's bodies, personal tendencies and associations. This is the portion of one's total Karma which has been chosen to bare fruit in the present life.

- *Kriyamana Karma*: The *karma* being created and added to *sanchita* in this life by one's thoughts, words, and actions or in the inner worlds between lives. While some *Kriyamani Karma*s bear fruit in the current life, others are stored for future births.

Karma is the driving force that brings the soul back again and again into human birth in the evolutionary cycle of transmigration called *samsara*. When all earthly *karma*s are resolved and the Self has been realized, the soul is liberated from rebirth.

Whether one believes in re-incarnation or not, there can be little argument about the law of causality in the physical world, and by extension in the spiritual world. As long as one holds a belief in a higher order of being, in some greater potential for all beings, then there is a need to pay attention to the actions that further the realization of the higher potential, and to avoid those actions which hinder this actualization.

It is important for all spiritual aspirants to realize that the practice of self-restraint and the development of moral character is critical to achieving the goal of Self-realization. Self-restraint is not merely a set of rules given by religious prophets or social reformers to control the masses, nor is it some ideal philosophical concept. In spiritual practice, self-restraint is the principal path to overcome the spiritual Law of *Karma*.

For each of the three kinds of *Karma* there is a different method of resolution. Nonattachment to the fruits of action, along with daily rites of worship and strict adherence to the codes of *dharma*, stops the accumulation of *kriyamana* or new *karmic* consequences. *Parabdha*

Karma is resolved only through being experienced and lived through, and cannot be bypassed. *Sanchita Karma,* the nascent store of *karmic* consequences is normally inaccessible, and can be burned away only through the grace and initiation [*diksha*] of the spiritual guide, who prescribes spiritual practice [*sadhana*]which generates spiritual heat and fire [*tapas*] for the benefit of the earnest spiritual seeker. Through the sustained *kundalini* heat of this *tapas,* the *karmic* seeds are fried, and therefore will never sprout in this or future lives.

Take to heart the words of Shri Yukteswar as reported by his disciple Paramhansa Yogananda:

> *Man is a soul and has a body. When he properly places his sense of identity, he leaves behind all compulsive pattern. So long as he remains confused in his ordinary state of spiritual amnesia, he will know the subtle fetters of environmental law.*

> *God is Harmony; the devotee who attunes himself will never perform any action amiss. His activities will be correctly and naturally timed to accord with astrological law. After deep prayer and meditation he is in touch with his divine consciousness; there is no greater power than that inward protection.*

> *All human ills arise from some transgression of universal law. The scriptures point out that man must satisfy the laws of nature, while not discrediting the divine omnipotence. He should say: 'Lord, I trust in Thee, and Thou can help me, but I too will do my best to undo any wrong I have done'. By a number of means – by prayer, by will power, by yoga meditation, by consultation with saints, by use of astrological bangles – the adverse effects of past wrongs can be minimized or nullified.*

Divine intervention is not necessary for the functioning of *karma* since it is a neutral, self-perpetuating law of the inner cosmos, much as gravity is an impersonal law of the outer cosmos. Just as a person who jumps off a twenty foot window is going to get hurt, so someone who acts in a negative way will have to suffer the effects of the negative *karma* - **there is no punishment by God**, it is the natural working of a law.

There is no sin or guilt, only forward or backward *karma* – terms describing actions leading the soul either toward or away from the spiritual goal of Self-Realization. In this way the only "sin" or *papa* is any action, word or thought that leads one away from the Divine. Since the Divine is Truth, every lie denies our divine nature and takes us away from the true Self.

Another way to look at the effects of our actions is to grade karma as: white [*sukla*], black [*krishna*], mixed [*sukla-krishna*], or niether white nor black [a*sukla-akrishna*]. The latter term describes the *karma* of the *jnani*, the man of wisdom who, as Rishi Patanjali says, is established in *kaivalya*, freedom from *prakriti* (bondage of matter) through realization of the Self. Similarly, one's own *karma* must be in a condition of *asukla-akrishna*, quescient balance, in order for liberation to be attained. The equivalence of *karma* is called *karmasamya*, and is a factor that brings *malaparipaka*, or maturity of the seed of negativity. It is this state of resolution in preparation for *samadhi* at death that all Hindus seek through making amends and settling differences.

Each of these types can be divided into two categories: arabdha (begun, undertaken – *karma* that is sprouting) and anarabdha (not commenced; dormant – that is seed *karma*). This is an important distinction because once a particular karma becomes *arabdha*, then it is no longer possible to destroy it and its effect has to run the course. It is only the seed karma that can be destroyed by the fire of spiritual practice.

Like the four-fold edict of *dharma*, the three-fold edict of *karma* has both individual and impersonal dimensions. Personal *karma* is thus influenced by broader contexts, sometimes known as family *karma*, community *karma*, national *karma*, global *karma* and universal *karma*. In this context, everyone born on Earth have some shared responsibility for the state of the world. It is no accident that certain people are born in a particular country or as part of a family – there are shared *karmic* bonds involved.

It is comforting to know that no matter how complicated our lives have been and how big a mountain of karmic debts are in our spiritual bank account, the great beings such as Lord Krishna who have led the way to Self-Realization also tell us that:

> *Even he with the worst of karma who ceaselessly meditates on Me quickly loses the effects of his past bad actions. Becoming a high-souled being, he soon attains perennial peace. Know this for certain: the devotee who puts his trust in Me never perishes.*
>
> *Bhagavad Gita 9. 30-31*

A pioneering spiritual Master of Kriya Yoga of our times Paramhansa Yogananda has identified the cause of our subjugation to the Law of Karma as the personal ego:

> *The iron filings of karma are attracted only where a magnet of the personal ego still exists.*

The Adi-Shankaracharya who revitalized the *sanatana dharma* during the past dark age was the great exponent of the vedantic philosophy. He has given the anti-dote to karma as Self-Realization:

> *When everything is known as the Self, not even an atom is seen as other than the Self.... As soon as knowledge of reality has sprung up, there can be no fruits of past actions*

to be experienced, owing to the unreality of the body, just as there can be no dream after waking.

As long as we struggle in ignorance of our True Self and under the control of the ego, we are subject to the Law of Karma, but once we realize our true nature, we transcend the necessity for the Law and all karmic consequences evaporate.

Maya in Saiva Siddhanta

Saiva Siddhanta is the name given to one of the principal religious philosophies in Southern India. It should be of particular interest to spiritual students as it constitutes the metaphysical ground for the goals and beliefs of the *Tamil Siddhas*. It is less well-known than the other philosophies that have been promulgated by *yogis*, such as Kashmiri Shaivism, Vedanta or the venerable Samkhya.

The origins of *Saiva Siddhanta* are shrouded in mystery and its basic tenets have been interpreted by the religious establishment, with barely restrained antipathy towards the "unorthodox" Siddhas, who usually acted from their own realized truth, rather than from dogma. Therefore, it has now assumed the form of a "religion" rather than the revelations of perfected beings who have seen reality.

Shaivism is the name given to the various schools of Indian Philosophy that designate "Shiva" (the Auspicious) as the immanent, transcendent, and ultimate principle, which creates, sustains, and dissolves the universe. The various schools of Shaivism are called *Trika*, because they share and utilize the three fundamental concepts of *pati*, *pasu*, and *pasa* to explain the relationship between the ultimate reality (*Shiva – Pati*), the individual souls (*atman – pasu*), and the limiting factors (*mala – pasa*) that restrict the powers of the souls.

The available historical evidence suggests that *Saiva Siddhanta* originated in Kashmir and was older and more popular than the philosophy of the Shiva Sutras of Vasugupta. The latter is now known as *Kashmir Shaivism*, due to its overwhelming dominance in that part of the world. The Karikas of Sadyojyoti (9th century C.E.) is one of the earliest extant descriptions of *Saiva Siddhanta*. By the tenth century C.E., we find that there has been a shift south to Madhya Pradesh, as shown by the works of Raja Bhoja of Dhar (1018-60 C.E.) Subsequently, the leadership moved further south, and has been established in Tamil Nadu, since 1200 C.E. by the Tamil saints, such as Aghora-Siva and Meykander.

Paradoxically, it appears that *Saiva Siddhanta* was actually brought south to Tamil Nadu, by Tirumoolar, who was previously known as Sundernath, and his magna opus of Siddha Yoga, the Tirumandirum, propounds *Saiva Siddhanta* philosophy, predating by centuries, the systematic treatment of the medieval Tamil Saints.

The later formulations of *Saiva Siddhanta* have led to its classification as a dualistic philosophy, as opposed to the monistic systems of *Vedanta* and the *Trika Kashmir Saivism*. Certainly, the predominant form of *Saiva Siddhanta*, which is prevalent in Tamil Nadu today is based on a dualistic model, but an unbiased interpretation of the Tirumandirum might possibly lead one to conclude that Tirumoolar was writing about a monistic form of *Saiva Siddhanta*. However, as time passed, control of its dogmatic formulation fell out of the hands of the Yogis or Siddhas, into the hands of religiously minded devotees, or *Bhaktas*, who did not practice Yoga.

It would be interesting to study whether the thesis that there is a distinct *yogic* or monistic form of *Saiva Siddhanta*, as represented by the Tirumandirum is tenable. The texts currently popular are of the religious or dualistic strain, as represented by the canonical texts such as the Tattva Prakasa of Bhoja, and the Sivajnanabodha of Meykandar. All interpretations are now colored by the assumption that this is a dualistic model and it would be difficult to find any expert who would look at it without that presumption.

It is well documented that many of the *siddhas* or yogis who are the heroes of the spiritually minded were persecuted and ridiculed by the religious establishment during the middle ages in Tamil Nadu. However, the *siddhas* gave their wisdom in mystically encrypted songs. These songs are still sung today by the masses with little understanding of the true import of their teachings. They have both an outer meaning and an inner esoteric meaning that can only be deciphered under the guidance of someone who has realized reality.

It is not my intent to give a tutorial in Saiva Siddhanta nor to trace its possible non-dualistic roots here. However, it would be interesting to compare how various yogic philosophies have approached the same topic.

One of the key divergences between the major philosophical systems is the treatment of the concept of *Maya*, and it would be instructive to first examine the various ways that this key concept has been dealt with.

In *Vedanta*, a non-Saiva system, *maya* and its world creation are unreal or *mithya*, just as the superposition of the image of a snake on a rope has no substance. The only reality is *Brahman*, and the appearance of *maya* is caused by the operation of *avidya* or ignorance.

In contrast to *Vedanta*, *Kashmir Shaivism* takes the position that *Maya* is a power or Sakti of Shiva, who creates the universe from Himself, by His own will. Since Shiva is real, *Maya* and the universe have to be real also. Shiva is the efficient, instrumental and material cause of the universe, and there can be no "other". The Pratyabhyjna-hrdaya [Sutra 3] states:

> *Para-Shiva is both immanent and transcendent to the universe. The universe is His manifestation within Himself. All of the Tattvas or categorical principles, from Shiva to Prithvi are within Himself.*

Orthodox or Dualistic *Saiva Siddhanta* does not belief that *maya* or the universe can be a part of the Shiva reality, and gives it a separate existence and reality, as a non-sentient matter, or *a-cit*. Only Shiva is *cit*, and by His power, *maya* is made to evolve the universe of experience, but Shiva is unaffected by and always separate from the impure world. Tattva-Prakasa of Bhoja states:

> *He is called Shiva as he is untouched by the beginning-less [anava] mala. He is uninvolved and above it all, but by his very presence the universe is created, as rice-grains are turned into food by the fire, though not touched by it.*

If one looks at this aspect, there is really no disagreement that the one True Reality, whether called Shiva or Brahman is unaffected by creation in all three models.

There is no difference even in whether the created universe is separate from the Lord or not. Since in Vedanta, the created universe is unreal; in Kashmire Shaivism, the universe is real but cannot be separated from the Lord; finally, in orthodox Saiva Siddhanta, the universe is made of separate inert matter, that only takes on life because of the power of the Lord, and so does not truly exist without the Lord.

In Tirumandirum, Tirumoolar would seem to take a view closer to *Kashmir Shaivism*, as regards *Maya*, making it an evolute from Siva, rather than a non-existent as in *Vedanta*, or a separate entity, as in Dualistic *Saiva Sidddhanta*. Verse 2341 of Tirumandirum states:

> *As fire and heat,*
> *Are Siva and Sakti,*
> *With Him as a substance,*
> *She, Jiva's awareness expands;*
> *Darkness and Light She is;*
> *She pervades the malas three;*
> *And then by Light of Grace,*
> *She makes Jiva the very Siva.*

The issue here would be whether Sakti is separate from Maya or is Maya dependent on Sakti because it is said in the Tirumandirum that:

The sun, the moon, agni and the celestials of the eight directions,
The space, water, air, and earth
The tanmatras, the karmendriyas and the antahkaranas
All these come out of maya along with bindu.

All creation has come from Maya. The orthodox dogma is that Maya is an inert matter from which the universe is created through Shakti by Shiva. An analogy often used is that Maya is the clay, Shakti is the turning wheel and Shiva is the potter that fashioned the clay into a pot. The only drawback is that the wheel is separate from the potter in the example whereas the Siddhantin would have us believe that Shakti is not different from Shiva. This is just as arbitrary as separating Maya from Shakti. It could just as easily be interpreted that Maya is another form of Shakti which is the power of Shiva – this would be the same position as Kashmiri Shaivism!

A further study of the Tirumandirum, and comparison with the dualistic stream of *Saiva Siddhanta*, with regards to other key concepts, such as the existence of individual souls, the causes of suffering, and the goal of life, will help elucidate the beliefs of one of the great Siddhas. It might also be instructive if the teachings of the other Siddhas can be interpreted as to their alignment with orthodoxy or otherwise.

Vedanta according to the Advaita

Vedanta is based on the Upanisads, which together with the Vedanta
Sutras and the Bhagavad Gita are regarded as authoritative texts.
However, since people have different temperaments and different
capacities for the truth, so different schools of philosophy have arisen
through the different interpretations by the leading commentators of
the Vedanta Sutras.

There are three main approaches taken in Vedanta. All three do not
subscribe to the Samkya philosophy of two separate and independent
realities. Madhava taught a dualistic model in which man and the universe
is ever separate from Brahman the God, but totally dependent on God
for its existence and the goal of man is to serve God and be established
in his grace. Ramanuja taught a qualified Monism in which man is a ray
or spark of God, and the goal is to become the creator of the Universe,
Lord Narayana, but still slightly separate from Brahman the Self-existent.
For Shankara, who taught the strict monism of Advaita, there is only
Brahman, and the goal of man is to realize his identity with Brahman.

Tat Tvam Asi is the final Self-realization according to Advaita because
Brahman or Pure Consciousness is the only Reality, and the universe
of names and forms is basically unreal, with man, in his true essence,
being one with the Being of Brahman.

The Advaitins consider the other two approaches to be stepping stones
to their model of Reality or Brahman. The first step is to approach
Reality as a devotional servant, and then closer as a junior partner, and
finally as identical. In this model, all difference and plurality is illusory.

The great expositor of Advaita is Adi Shankaracharya. In his
interpretation, Supreme Brahman is impersonal and is not an object
and cannot be bounded by descriptions. Para-Brahman is not only
timeless, spaceless, and attributeless, It is also infinite, all-full, and self-
existent. In Brahman there is no distinction between substance and

attribute. Sat-Chit-Ananda or Existence-Consciousness-Bliss is the very essence of Brahman, not just a property or attribute.

One of the Powers of Brahman is Maya, which does not have a separate existence. Through this power of Maya, Saguna (with form or attributes) Brahman apparently arises, but this is not separate from Nirguna or formless Brahman.

Through the Power of Maya, the world arises. The world is not a total illusion, but neither is it absolutely real. The world according to Shankara is only relatively real. The unchanging Brahman appears as the changing world through the mysterious Maya and so the real is hidden by the unreal. However, only when true knowledge appears, will the real be realized and the unreal disappear. This superposition of the world on Brahman is called ignorance or *avidya*.

Shankara calls the individual soul Jiva but in reality Jiva is only the eternal Soul Atman covered by a veil of illusion. The mistaken Jiva(s) is/are identical with the Atman, which itself cannot be established by extraneous proofs because it is self-evident and is the essence of the very one that denies it. The Atman is the basis of all knowledge. The individuality of the Jiva lasts only so long as it is subject to unreal limiting conditions or *upadhis* imposed by *avidya* or ignorance, which in turn arises by the power of Maya.

The Jiva identifies itself with the body, mind and the senses and in this delusion, it thinks, acts and enjoys. However, just as when the bubble bursts, it becomes one with the ocean, or when the pot breaks, the space inside and outside becomes one, so does the Jiva become one with Atman which is one with Brahman. When the knowledge of Brahman dawns and the darkness of ignorance is annihilated, the slavery of Individuality vanishes and only the Infinite Freedom of Sat-Chit-Ananda Is.

To understand better the relative reality of the world, the theory of superposition is useful. Just as a snake is superimposed on a rope in the twilight, but the rope is not changed in any way by this illusion, so the superposition of the world on Brahman, by the power of Maya and state of *avidya*, does not change It in anyway. Once you see that it is an illusion, the snake vanishes, just as Brahman is realized without any change or transformation. Just as fear vanishes when the rope is seen, so does the suffering of the world disappear when Brahman is realized. The Atman is not affected by the phenomena of the world.

According to Shankara, Liberation or Moksha is the merging of the individual soul in Brahman, through the means of dismissing the false knowledge or error of separation. He taught a practical Vedanta, using Karma Yoga or Action and Bhakti or Devotion, as well as the Self-enquiry or Jnana Yoga.

Brahman is the Ultimate Knowledge. Brahman is the Ultimate and Only Knower. Brahman is the Knowing or Process of Gnosis, and the only means of attaining immortality. All physical and mental phenomena originate from an aspect of Divinity called Isvara or Brahman-with-attribute and its power of Maya.

Through Self-enquiry, one experiences the reality that the Self is not the body, breath, mind or intellect. Pain and pleasure are only passing and changing modes of the body, senses and mind, born from Maya operating in the personal level as *avidya* or ignorance, and therefore are ultimately unreal. The Self is realized as existence-knowledge-bliss.

Even though it is only through Maya that the Eternal nature of the Self is veiled, and the individual self misconstrues the world and itself as being different from Brahman, Maya is indescribable. Maya is neither real, nor unreal, nor both real and unreal. It is not real because it does not have any independent existence apart from Brahman. It is not unreal because it is the actual power by which Brahman manifests itself as the apparent universe. It is also not both real and unreal because this would be self-contradictory. From the viewpoint of the world,

Maya is experienced as real, but from the standpoint of Absolute Reality, it is unreal. However, even though it is indescribable, Maya is removable. By right knowledge or proper understanding, the misunderstanding called Maya is removed.

The misunderstanding which is responsible for all human sufferings, actually makes no difference to the Self, which is pure and unaffected by the laws, rules and regulations of the World. Paradoxically, this misunderstanding causes one to lose one's awareness of perpetual happiness and bliss. Liberation is not so much an achievement, it is rather the realization of the Truth that already abides within.

Accordingly, no one is perfect or imperfect. No one is successful or unsuccessful. There is no such thing as liberation or bondage.

A story is used to illustrate the illusory nature of bondage and liberation. Once there was a man who owned a donkey, and one day he pretended to tie the donkey to a stake by showing the donkey the loose end of the rope around its neck and then only pretending to tie it to the stake. The next day, he sent his son to bring the donkey to him, but the donkey would not budge, not even when the boy started to beat it with a stick. When the man heard about this from his son, he laughed and going to the donkey, took the rope and moved his hand around at the stake as if untying the knot. Only then would the donkey move.

In actuality all of us are ever-free, but our imagination create bondage for us and prevent us from releasing our self-tied bonds. All spiritual practices are like the process demonstrated by the donkey's master.

Vedanta provides a systematic method of spiritual practice which helps one to gain release from the self-created imaginary rope of bondage. First, there is the study of scriptures and listening to learned teachers so as to understand the nature of the external objects and the essential nature of the self. Then comes contemplation on the truths learned in the first step. Finally, one applies the truths in one's daily life. One must form a lifestyle in which he can maintain his true consciousness.

The sages of the Upanishads who have experienced Reality have all proclaimed:

> *The world is an illusion.*
> *Brahman is the only Reality.*
> *Knowing this I abide in eternal peace,*
> *for I am all-pervading immortal Atman.*
> *Never was I born. Never will I die.*
> *I am ever free. I am perfect.*
> *I am pure. I am independent.*

The concepts of Vedanta are a great gift to those still harboring the self-imposed misunderstanding of identification with the body, mind and senses. They can give the confidence to act in expanding one's understanding of one's relationship to the world and to Reality. Vedenta calls upon all of us to care and dare to live large.

Parable 5: Is This Real?

Long ago, the great divine seer or *rishi* Vasishtha was instructing the solar prince Rama, as recorded in the Yoga Vasishtha.

The sage said: "The mind does not have an independent existence. Just as the waves are dependent on the waters of sea, so also the mind is dependent on the Divine. The mind is ever changing. Sometimes it takes a friend to be a foe, and other times a foe for a friend. It brings the great to a low level and exalts the low to a high level. It has one feeling or state at one time and another feeling or state at another time. It takes the truth for untruth and untruth for truth. Pleasure and pain, joy and grief, happiness and sorrow are the creations of the mind only. The mind alone reaps the fruits of good and evil actions. There is no perception of an object independent of the mind. The mind is the cause of all its feelings. You hear, feel, see, taste and smell through the mind only. It is the mind that moves this body. Time, distance, place; length, breadth and height; quickness, slowness, greatness and smallness; too much or too little; blackness or redness - all these arise only in the mind. They all belong to the mind proper.

Thoughts of objects lead to bondage. Renunciation of thoughts leads to emancipation. This universe is nothing but the expansion of thoughts. This world is a big show. This show is kept up by the mind only. Just as the seasons produce the changes in the trees, so also the mind causes differences in the disposition of human beings. There are as many minds as there are men in this world. It is difficult to find two men of one mind.

The mind sports in objects. It creates illusion. Through the play of the mind nearness appears to be great distance and great distance appears to be nearness. An age seems to be a moment and vice versa. To illustrate this idea well, I shall narrate to you now a very interesting story. O Rama! Hear this with rapt attention."

Lavana, a descendant of King Harishchandra, ruled over the country of Uttar Pandava. He was a glorious and virtuous king. He was once seated on his throne in his golden palace. All his ministers and officers were present. There appeared at this time a *siddha*, a perfected *yogi*. He bowed to the King and exclaimed: "O my lord! Let me show you my magical powers."

The *siddha* waved his bunch of peacock feathers. A messenger from the king of the neighboring lands entered the court with a horse like that of the king of the gods and said: "O lord! My master has made a present of this horse to you."

The *siddha* requested the King to mount the horse and ride it for his pleasure. The King stared at the horse and his body was seen to relax. After some more time his body fell on the ground as if in a faint. Alarmed, the courtiers lifted the body. Then the King came back to normal consciousness.

The ministers and courtiers became very anxious and enquired of the King: 'What is the matter with Your Majesty?"

The King said; "The Siddha waved his bunch of peacock feathers. I saw a horse before me. I mounted the horse and rode in a desert in the hot sun. My tongue was parched. I was quite fatigued. Then I reached a beautiful forest. While I was riding the horse, a creeper encircled my neck and the horse ran away. I rocked to and fro in the air throughout the night with the creeper around my neck. I shivered with extreme cold.

The day dawned and I saw the sun. I cut the creeper that encircled my neck. I then beheld a girl carrying some food and water in her hands. I was very hungry and asked her to give me some food. She did not give me anything. I followed her closely for a long time. She then turned to me and said: "I am a peasant, if you promise to marry me in my own place before my parents and live with me there, I will give you what I have in my hand this very moment." I agreed to marry her. She then gave me half of the food. I ate the food and drank the beverage of jambu fruits.

Then she took me to her father and asked his permission to marry me. He consented. She took me to her abode. The father of the girl killed monkeys, crows and pigs for flesh and dried them on strings of nerves. A small shed was erected. I had my seat on a big plantain leaf. My squint-eyed mother-in-law then looked at me with her blood-red eyeballs and said: "Is this our would-be son-in-law?"

The marriage festivities began with great merriment. My father-in-law presented me with clothes and other articles. Drink and meat were freely distributed. The meat-eating natives began to beat their drums. The girl was given to me in marriage. I was renamed Pushta. The wedding festival lasted for seven days. A daughter was first born of this union. She brought forth again a boy in the course of three years. She again gave birth to a daughter. I became an old man with a large family and lived for a long time. Children are a source of grief. The miseries of human beings which arise out of passion take the form of a child. My body became old and emaciated on account of family cares and worries. I had to undergo pain through heat and cold in that dreary forest. I was clad in old and ragged clothes. I carried loads of firewood on my head. I was exposed to the chill winds. I had to live upon roots. I thus spent sixty years of my life as if they were so many ages of long duration. Then there was a severe famine. Many died of starvation. Some of my relatives left the place.

My wife and I left this country and walked in the hot sun. I carried two children on my shoulders and the third on my head. After walking a long distance I arrived at the fringe of a forest. We all took a little rest under a big palmyra tree. My wife expired on account of the long travel in the hot sun. My younger son, Pracheka, rose up and, standing before me and with tears gushing out of his eyes, said: "Papa, I am hungry, give me immediately some meat and drink or else I shall die."

He repeatedly said with tears in his eyes that he was dying of hunger. I was then moved by paternal affection. I was very sorely afflicted at heart. Unable to bear the distress, I made up my mind to put an end to my life by falling into fire. I collected some wood, heaped them together and set fire to them.

As I stood up to jump into the fire, I fell down from my throne and woke up to hear the sound of the musical instruments and see you lifting me and shouting the words "Jaya, Jaya! (victory to thee!"). I now find myself as King Lavana but not as a peasant native. I understand now that it was the *siddha* that had put me through all these imaginary troubles for so long a period.

The ministers enquired as to the identity of the *siddha* but it was found that he had disappeared completely.

Vasishtha then explained: "O Rama! This *siddha* is no other than the divine Maya (Power of Universal Illusion.) This story clearly illustrates that this universe is not other than the mind itself. Para Brahman Himself appears as the mind and the world. Whatever you see is a manifestation of chit (consciousness) only. Time is but a mode of the mind. In dream you experience the events of a century within five minutes. When the mind is concentrated, an hour appears as five minutes. If there is no concentration, ten minutes appear as three hours. Everybody has experienced this in this world. Within a few minutes King Lavana had the experience of sixty years.

This universe is a creation of the mind. Mind or Maya is the greatest juggler or magician. Mind or Maya represents the *siddha* or the magician of the above story. Mind is Maya. Mind is the instrument of Maya. The experiences of King Lavana represent the miserable condition of human beings who are slaves to desires and cravings and the state of the world. This illusory world is only a display of the infinite power or omnipotence of the Lord – all beings experience the unrealities. The real is unreal for them. Just as the tree is extended by the expansion of its boughs and branches, so also the mind is enlarged by the various inventions of its imagination.

If you destroy the *sankalpas* or imaginations of the mind, if you discipline the mind in a perfect manner, if you bring the mind gradually under your control through discrimination, enquiry, dispassion, and regular meditation on the Atman (True Self), then you will not be overpowered by Maya. You will attain immortality and enjoy the eternal bliss of the Infinite."

The Power of Discrimination

Discrimination is a translation of the Sanskrit term Viveka, which is used in various ways in many yogic texts that deal with consciousness. What is the purpose of discussing this term today? It is to introduce a pivotal process that leads to liberation. You might wonder....liberation from what?

The state of liberation varies with the type of philosophical model, which you are following. To those who follow dualistic Samkya, it might be realization of the identity with the Real Consciousness called Purusha, and total freedom from the affects of the Real Matter Prakriti. To *Patanjali*, it might be cessation of the afflictions, which cause the modifications of the consciousness. To the Advaitins, it might be the realization of the identity with Brahman, and freedom from the veils of Maya. However, the common point is the freedom from the law of cause and effect or the governance of *Karma*.

Discrimination is a power of the higher mind that allows us to achieve liberation from all *karmic* consequences. *Patanjali* has said in his Sutras: "The Knowledge born of discrimination is liberating, non-sequential and (inclusive) of all conditions and all times."

This means that discrimination leads to a state, which is not limited by time and space. Acts done in the past does not have to play out its consequences any more.

Shankara, in his Crest Jewel of Discrimination points out that:
"Neither by weapons, by any scripture, by fire, or by water, can this tree of ignorance be hewn down; nor by millions of different kinds of works can it be hewn down. Only the great sword of discrimination can cut down this Maya, and that sword should be whetted by the grace of the Lord."

Discrimination can be practiced at different levels. In the first stage, it may be as simple as distinguishing what is helpful on the spiritual path, and what can be hindrances, and choosing the helpful. For example, taking drugs that damage the nervous system and lead to addiction is not conducive to achieving Self-Realization.

Next, discrimination can be practiced towards the afflicted fluctuations of consciousness, because the thoughts and feelings arising from them lead to suffering, while the perception of the *karmic* consequences of strengthening the web of desires through thoughts, speech and actions can break the causal chain of ignorance.

It is necessary to distinguish the permanent from the transitory, the real from the relatively real or unreal, the Self from the world. Discrimination is a constant, continuous and focused practice of awareness of the true versus the untrue – the *dharmic* versus the *adharmic*.

In the early stages, discrimination will give rise to fear and disillusion with ordinary experience:

> *To the people who have developed discrimination, all is misery on account of the pains resulting from change, anxiety and tendencies, as also on account of the conflicts between the functioning for the gunas and the vrittis of the mind.*
>
> Patanjali Yoga Sutras

What is the process of discrimination?
To *Patanjali*, it is the practice of the eight limbs of Yoga, by which the impurities dwindle away and there dawns the light of wisdom leading to discriminative discernment.

After the stage of fear and disillusion, discrimination gives rise to the Light of spiritual illumination, which guides the aspirant through the path. By the continuous awareness of reality, ignorance is overcome, and the emergence of new *karma* is prevented. The "unceasing vision

186

of discernment" is achieved when there is total identification with the Self in *asmaprajnatah samadhi*. Finally in conjunction with *Vairagya*, or dispassion or non-attachment, the state of Dharma-megha-Samadhi is realized, and the seeds of previous *karma*s are "burnt".

Shankara has given the formula for freedom: "The wise man should discriminate between the Self and the non-self in order to be free."

Even the meditative are conscious of the external world, because of *karma*, the result of past actions. As long as one feels pleasure and pain, so long *karma* remains; but the knowledge of "Atman Brahman" does away with all past actions done in millions and millions of births.

The process is meditative awareness of the Self, leading to absorption, leading to identification. Discriminative Knowledge is the key to freedom.

All the great spiritual traditions of India are based in the concept of *dharma* or natural law. *Dharma* refers to ultimate righteousness and the collective laws of truth that govern the universe. *Dharma* sees that righteousness prevails and moves us forward in growth and spiritual evolution.

Let us apply our discriminative faculty and consider the relationship between *dharma* and *karma*: The most important *dharmic* law is the Law of Karma: as we act, so must we experience the fruits of our actions....or we reap what we sow....not only in this life, but in future lives as well. There is absolute justice in this universe, but this occurs through many incarnations and cannot be seen by what is happening in the moment. It is not only a justice of outer rewards and punishments but also one in the evolution of consciousness. Flowing throughout all of one's lives and all of life's circumstances is the soul intelligence, which is working towards removing the ignorance and suffering in which we live.

It is our experience that a *dharmic* action will provide inner peace and happiness and allows us to pursue spiritual practice. *Adharmic* action constricts our consciousness and brings confusion to the mind, even if it gives us some momentary pleasure or gain. We need to recognize that the external conditions of life are normally what are best for inner development, whatever that may entail, even if it is very difficult. When we are at a crossroads however, we can turn to *dharma* and discrimination to make the choice for us. *Dharma* is reflected in situations when ultimately everyone benefits. The key is having discrimination enough to clearly see the Truth in the situation.

Discrimination is the ability to discern the real from the unreal. It is only by means of discrimination that all our doubts can be eliminated eventually. Under all circumstances, the spiritual seeker should maintain an awareness of the underlying reality governing all phenomena.

Nothing happens to us by chance, coincidence or accident. Other people do not have the power to impose their own misunderstandings upon our own *karma*. Whatever happens to us is the result of *karmic* effects - it corresponded to *samskaras* (habitual reaction or the seeds of *karma*). *Karma* is said to be the result of making wrong choices over and over and over which creates a momentum. These choices are reflections of our *samskaras*, the negative habitual emotions and behaviors, which take over the personality and move it onward into creating and living out more *karma*. It is not possible to identify the first case, *karma* or *samskara* – the chicken or the egg.

Holding onto negative habit patterns such as anger, envy, guilt, or worry, whatever it may be simply sets up the *karmic* conditions for those feelings to reoccur over an over again in our lives. You can take control over *karma*s, by the decisions and choices you make, at any given moment. The choice is the free will you have in how you are going to think about something. You have freewill, which determines how you are going to react to something.

It is counterproductive to hold on to an emotion. It doesn't help anyone else, or even the score, it simply causes us pain, by being a degenerating influence upon our perception and experience in the present and in the future. If your wish to be rid of a *samskara*, you should commit yourself to surrendering it to the Divine and make the effort to let of it.

Having discrimination, desiring to see the truth in each situation and having the detachment to let go of old selfish desires can help you set new priorities. Our present state is based on our previous priorities and desires. So ask yourself if what you have is what you want? As long as an old priority still motivates us, it will be an obstacle to further growth and expansion.

In order to progress in our growth, we must first take responsibility for our own emotions. No one else is the cause of the way we feel. In the same way, we must not blame ourselves for the way someone else feels. If we know in our heart that we have not done anything to hurt someone and we are just being ourselves and living our lives as truthfully as we can, then we need not accept blame that someone else might want to impose upon us.

We cannot control how other people react to a situation. However, negative energies from other people need not have anything to do with us - they are simply venting their feelings at the time and we just happen to be around. We have control over how we react to these energies. We can use our discriminative faculty to see if there is any obvious reason why we've attracted such negative energy, or why it is affecting us. We can look at what aspect of a criticism is true. By looking at how others are reacting to us, we may have an insight into our own *samskaras*, or our own unconscious ways of relating to people.

We should also make the conscious choice to take responsibility for everything that we do. Remember it is our *dharma* to do whatever is necessary to maintain our own state, whatever it takes to remain undisturbed within. Some of us subject ourselves to negativities because we don't want to hurt someone else's feelings. But emotional negativity is very draining - it can be very weakening if we have not learned to bring our own highest state into a situation. It is not being compassionate to deal with another's negativity. We don't owe that to someone. It is something they will ultimately have to deal with and purify within themselves.

The key to dissolving all negativities is forgiveness. If we do not forgive someone, then we carry the weight and power of that lack of forgiveness within ourselves. We are the ones who are being affected by it. The person we can't forgive simply experiences his or her own feeling. Our lack of forgiveness affects us in a negative way. We must learn to forgive *samskaras* in others and in ourselves. Forgiveness is very purifying and very powerful.

Whenever we have to make life-changing decisions we can turn to *dharma* and discrimination to make the choice for us. Once we begin to take responsibility for everything that we do we begin to see the Truth in each situation, not what we would like to see, but the truth as it is. If we are sincere in wanting the right thing then we are aligned with the Truth. There is always the best path to take – the right thing to do.

We soon realize that *karma* is what lies behind whatever happens in our lives – it is our *karma*, not some capricious semi-divine being's joke or someone's else's fault. It is the movement of Time that activates the working of our *karma*. By following our *dharma*, we achieve peace with our *karma*. It is our *dharma* to go through our *karma* with awareness. We can't do anything about our *karma*, which manifests at this moment. But if we deal with our *karmic* situation in each moment with acceptance, we can be in harmony with it. This is what *sadhana* or spiritual practice is all about: to live our lives in harmony no matter what happens.

When anything happens, it is our *sadhana* to achieve harmony with it. It is a sign of growth when we can experience our *karma* without justifying it, or rejecting it or feeling pride in it, and simply remain undisturbed and maintain a peaceful, loving inner state. *Samskaras* break through whenever we lose touch with our inner state. If we come into harmony with our *karma*, then we can break free from the influence of our *samskaras* and living free from the influence of *samskaras* is what liberation is all about. Then we are free to act spontaneously and in tune with Divine will all the time, no longer at the constant mercy of the fears and suffering associated with our past programs.

Let us live in dharma. Let us see the Truth in all things at all times. We must be willing to live simply and spontaneously with whatever is happening in our lives at any moment. We must give up our need to be separate and isolated and live as part of the whole, a state of being with all. Let is be at home wherever we are.

It is the power of discrimination which will enable us to overcome our karma by the path of dharma. Without discrimination, we are like a blind man without his trusty seeing-eye dog, and will blunder from one accident to another. By the aid of discrimination, we can avoid the pitfalls and get to our destination.

Truth, Error and Tolerance

How can we know the Truth? To the yogis, Truth is the direct realization of reality as it is. This direct realization requires a mode of knowing that has not been developed by or is not accessible to the majority of humanity. It is a super-conscious mode of knowing or awareness that develops with the practice of Kriya Yoga or other similar yogic disciplines focusing on Self-Realization.

To those who have not attained to the super-conscious states of knowing, truth as commonly understood is something that can be apprehended by the by five senses and/or comprehended by the mind. This is a conscious mode of knowing.

What then can we accept as true? All truths are verifiable. In our present limited state of knowing, all truths must be verified, because in this conscious mode of knowing, there is an element of error. Wise men have cautioned and consoled us that "to err is human!"

There are certain accepted methods employed to ascertain truth:
- Direct sense perception
- Indirect inference
- Reliable witness

The first is through the senses. This method should give us the greatest confidence. However, can we really belief our senses? Even our common experience will have convinced us that our sensory perception is error prone. This is because there needs to be corollary factors for the senses to function properly – proper lighting for good vision, short distance or high volume for good hearing etc. There also is the factor of mental interpretation that accompanies every sensory activity – the same drink may taste right for one person and be too sweet for another – who is right?

The sages use the famous example of the rope and the snake: you are returning home on a dark moonless night and see something white in the middle of the road. It looks like a snake (there are plenty of them in the country side where you live), and you stop fearfully. Just then the moon peeks out from the dark clouds and you see with great relief that is only a rope. The object hasn't changed, only our perception of it.

The second method is using the mind to make inferences to arrive at the truth. For example, it generally and universally accepted that 'where there is smoke, there is fire.' So, if you see smoke rising from the mountain, you may rightfully claim that the mountain is on fire. However, there may be alternative explanations – it could be someone sending smoke signals, or another burning object such as a car or garbage. In our technology age, special effects can generate the appearance of smoke from smoky vapor, without the agency of fire. Therefore all inferences also need to be verified because the mind cannot directly apprehend the truth without sensory verification – you need to go to the mountain and observe the cause of the smoke.

It is also true that minds are prone to error. Not every mind is well-trained in making logical inferences. There is variability in the quality of minds. The mind is also error prone because of its preconceptions and emotional predispositions. No normal mind is free from prejudice. The consequence is that we make biased inferences. When we see a beautiful blonde woman struggling with a particular task, we may jump to the conclusion that she is a "dumb blonde", when the actual case maybe that the task is not appropriate and anyone would struggle with it. There is a prejudice that "beautiful people" are "good" and "ugly people" are "bad," even though our experience would indicate otherwise – that there may not be a correlation between physical appearance and virtuous behavior.

The third mode of knowing the truth is through a reliable witness. If someone you know and trusts tells you that he saw a mutual friend in Hong Kong last week, you may confidently assert this fact and try to ascertain if she is back from the trip. However, such a truth still has to be verified, because the witness may be mistaken. A truly reliable witness would be one who cannot make a mistake, and only a sage can lay claim to such a state.

In this Internet age, the blessing is that there is an abundance of information, even an over-abundance. However, the curse is that there is a lot of misinformation – some deliberate or just plain prejudiced "information," while others are just mistakes being propagated at Internet speed. Most people would be unwilling to try to verify every piece of information being passed off as facts these days, through the various communication media – Internet, television, newspaper, radio, magazines and books. The consequence is that they become loaded with misinformation and prejudice.

It is ironic that given the situation that there are so many external and internal sources of error that most people believe they are the guardians of the truth and those that disagree or hold to a different position are by definition wrong. This "laziness" to examine and verify our truths has led to a very polarized and prejudiced society.

The sages of India have always recognized the flawed nature of conscious knowing, and have advocated tolerance to save us from the consequence of our errors.

Recently I read reports of a professor from the University of Colorado who was supposed to have compared the victims of the 9/11 terror attack to the Nazis who died in World War II. I do not know if this is an accurate representation of his words – if it is, then he should have our sympathy because it would be an indication of an unsound mind. However, what struck me most was that during an enquiry of his behavior, his supporters maintained a constant barrage of shouting and abusive physical behavior to prevent any kind of debate or dialog. This unwillingness to see both sides of a position is symptomatic of a prejudiced mind, not an open and enquiring mind.

An open and enquiring mind is a tolerant mind. Tolerance is a mark of humanity – and intolerance is a mark of inhumanity. It is not a call to stand by while manifest evil is taking place. It is not a call to tolerate the genocide in different parts of Africa, such as Rwanda. Tolerance is not apathy. It is an active behavior seeking to constantly ascertain the truth amid changing circumstances, verifying all facts and taking appropriate action at the right time.

Tolerance is based on mutual respect – it cannot be a one-sided virtue. Conflict arises when either party seeks to impose their viewpoints or prejudices on the other. When one side takes a majority role in society, and decides to "re-shape" or "purify" their society of dissidence, then mass violence results.

Society has a role to play to ensure that illegal, immoral or unethical behavior is not sanctioned, and its members protected from those that seek to harm them. However, even societies must recognize that legality, morality and ethical standards can change, and not take intolerance to a degree that cannot be remedied. Society does not have a mandate to regulate the views or harmless actions of its members.

It is ironic that as the world has become accessible to its inhabitants to a degree unheard of in many millennia, acceptance of the different norms within different societies is still far from catching up. Tolerance between societies holding different norms of behavior is critical to the continuance of the human race on this earth of ours. Intolerance will lead to war with its consequent unacceptable loss of lives on a huge scale. Just as individuals can be wrong, so can societies, as a whole.

Tolerant individuals lead to tolerant societies, which lead to a safer and happier world. Each one of us has a duty to examine our cherished values, respect those of others, and be willing to discuss or debate varying positions. Until Self-Realization is achieved, our truths may not be the Truth, and we can and will make mistakes. Tolerance ensures that our mistakes do not lead to dire negative consequences that cannot be reversed.

Tolerance is the beginning of Wisdom. It is the awareness that our present tools of knowing are not perfect, and that we need not be fearful of all truths. It is the willingness to open the mind to all sides of the truth.

Guidance from the Stars

During my twenties, I developed a great interest and facility in astrology, so much so, that I would frequently provide guidance and counsel to those who sought my help. It is not my goal to discuss the merits of this science which has been verified and testified to by ancient seers and yogis for thousands of years. Inept practitioners and prejudiced unscientific "scientists" have brought this noble science to disrepute. However, as Sir Isaac Newton responded to another member of the Royal Society, when his trust in astrology was denigrated, "Sir, I've studied it, you have not."

My goal is to discuss how this most ancient science can bring light to spiritual seekers and what role it can play. It is not to convince anyone of its efficacy or scientific basis.

As I progressed in my spiritual practices or *sadhana*, there was little time left for other pursuits. Being a householder, family responsibilities had to be assumed. I began to disdain astrology and totally dropped it from my consciousness during my thirties and forties, taking heart and courage from the words of Sri Yukteswar as reported by Yoganandaji, "The deeper the Self-realization of a man, the more he influences the whole universe by his subtle spiritual vibrations, and the less he himself is affected by the phenomenal flux."

In the last few years, as I've observed so many spiritual seekers struggling with their lives and circumstances, I've been moved to help them ease some of their suffering and give guidance on overcoming obstacles, so that they can continue on their paths to self realization.

What can be done through knowledge of one's birth-map or horoscope? Again, Sri Yukteswar tells us, "A child is born on that day and at that hour when the celestial rays are in mathematical harmony with his individual *karma*. His horoscope is a challenging portrait, revealing his unalterable past and its probable future results. But the natal chart can be rightly interpreted only by man of intuitive wisdom: these are few."

As the principle of *karma* has been explained in detail previously, it is only necessary to remember that not only is it the complete record of all our thoughts, words and deeds, as well as the law of cause and effect, it is also the mechanism which ensures the proper connection between the two.

The physical body carries it's karma in the genetic code – a map of physical potentials and limitations. The energy centers in the energy body are limited by the karma brought into the present life. Finally the mental body carries the tendencies and mental programs called *samskaras*. Scientists are now unraveling the human genome and can tell if a person has tendencies towards specific diseases.

In a similar fashion, the ancients looked at the skies and unraveled the cosmic star maps. From a person's natal horoscope, it is possible to tell the tendencies towards specific diseases and much more. Energetic, emotional and mental tendencies are all revealed and when placed against the earthly field of action, the likely occurrences of events can also be forecasted. For against these tendencies is superimposed the starry timeline (after all, we measure time by the movement of the sun and moon).

Of course, if it was only given to providing forecasts Indian Astrology would be of little value, for what will happen, will happen and what won't, won't. The glory of Jyotish is that there are remedies provided to offset negative events and promote positive events.

Many different types of remedies have been discovered, from the wearing of gems stones to the ingestion of herbs. The most powerful remedies are the mantras or vibration of power. These remedies can help to offset or deflect the effects of *karma*. If someone was going to break a leg, he may instead twist it. It is usually impossible to totally deny the power of *karma* coming to fruition.

Another use of the Heavenly map is for better understanding of our tendencies – strengths and weakness. This is a great aid in developing the *niyama* of *swadaya* or self-study. It is the true Jyotish, to dispel the darkness and ignorance from our minds.

I've been able to give guidance to students on the right type of *sadhana* or practices that they should pursue according to their *dharma*. It is possible to see the best cosmic energy or deity to connect with for liberation or the right mantra for transcendence.

We must not let our pride prevent us from taking advantage of such invaluable knowledge: "It is only when a traveler has reached his goal that his is justified in discarding his maps. During the journey, he takes advantage of any convenient short cut."

Sometimes, without having recourse to a horoscope, it is also possible to provide similar spiritual guidance from "seeing" the causal body of the spiritual seeker. It is my experience that when this has been done and then later compared with the results from the horoscope, there are remarkable concurrences. However, it is better to make use of astrology since a horoscope can provide a road-map that the spiritual aspirant can learn from at later periods and throughout one's life.

A cautionary note is in order: *karma* cannot be denied – we must reap the fruits of our actions. What is possible, is to channel and fashion the flow of the *karmic* retribution in less harmful ways. This is a delicate balancing act and generally will require effort from the person involved to take an active role, rather than a passive role.

The following words on Fate and Free will from Sri Aurobindo is highly instructive:

> *Someone is there who has determined; something is there which is Fate, let us say, the stars are only indicators. The astrologers themselves say that there are two forces, Daiva*

and Puruskara, fate and individual energy, and the individual energy can modify and even frustrate fate. Moreover, the stars often indicate several possibilities: for example that one may die in mid-age, but that if that determination can be overcome, one can live to a predictable old age. Finally, cases are seen in which predictions of the horoscope fulfill themselves with great accuracy up to a certain age, then they apply no more. This often happens when the subject turns away from the ordinary to the spiritual life."

Why Good People Do Bad Things

The other day I read that a group of our soldiers in Iraq may have deliberately killed some innocent civilians including women and children. This was very shocking since they were there to safeguard the liberty of the Iraqis and were representing the decent average American people. This was not a lone deranged individual but a concerted effort by a number of highly trained soldiers. How could they have done such a terrible deed?

The word for such an action against non-combatants is atrocity, and atrocities in wartime have been recorded since time immemorial. The Torah records the destruction of many peoples by the Jewish warriors taking the "promised land." The Iliad extols the atrocities by the Greek warriors against the Trojans and vice versa. In recent times, the Nazis committed atrocities against the Jewish people in the lands they conquered during World War II. During the Vietnam War, US soldiers have been responsible for reprehensible actions also. All these soldiers were otherwise decent people before they went to war.

Coming closer to home. What about Police brutality? Stories about ordinary policemen going beyond the law and striking out at those they are supposed to protect surface now and then.

I'm remembering that there were experiments done by some university professor on how the highly educated students would react under conditions where they were called upon to inflict pain and harm to their fellow students. The students were taken to one room where there was an instrument with a slider that they were told actually controlled another instrument in the second room that would inflict pain on someone connected to it. They were given some excuse that would justify the use of pain on the test subject – in reality the professor's assistant.

Each student in turn was given the task of activating the instrument of pain, when ordered by the professor. The students would hear the simulated screams from the test subject. Many of the students continued to inflict pain past what they were told was the threshold for permanent damage. The good news was that about 60% of the students refused. The bad news was that about 40% obeyed.

So what's going on? It was a study on how authority can force ordinary people to perform negative actions. It is well-known that in situations where authority is oppressive such as in communist countries of the past, children have been made to betray even their parents. Soldiers obey their commanders and will perform horrific actions as may have happened in Vietnam.

Authority figures include parents at home, teachers at school, bosses at work and government officials. We are told to obey them for various reasons and this sets up a conditioning of our responses. It is difficult to disobey an order from what we accept as an authority figure.

Another strange phenomenon is the hazing in school fraternities where students do harsh things to their fellow students. There is no designated authority in such cases, since it is a peer group. Students who want to join the group are made to strip and perform demeaning and sometimes dangerous activities under the supervision and obvious delight of their fellow students.

This is an example of peer pressure that can lead someone to agree to and carry out actions that they would otherwise find unethical, immoral or harmful to their fellow human beings. If someone wishes to belong to the group, they have to conform.

Returning to the soldiers in Iraq and the alleged atrocity that began this discussion, there is no indication that they were ordered to perform the killings. In fact, it is alleged they did the killings out of revenge or frustration at the death of one or more of their group. This may indicate a third stimulus for good people to do bad things. When someone is put in stressful conditions day in and day out, their behavior may become altered and their sense of right and wrong mitigated. These soldiers were under a lot of stress with daily attrition on their friends by terrorists that they could not find or fight. The stress may have led them to strike out blindly at innocent people.

However, given all these considerations, we must remember that not everyone blindly obeys authority, or buckles under peer pressure or gives in to anger under stress.

This leads one to consider the latent tendencies that are hidden in all of us. These latent tendencies are called *samskaras* and are from the results of our actions from past lives. They lie hidden in the causal body until the proper stimulus can ignite them into prominence and can cause a person to act out of character. An otherwise kind man or woman who has repressed their sexuality for many years may under conditions where he or she has control and authority over under-age persons, suddenly develop shocking thoughts that may overwhelm them to perform terribly wrong things to gratify themselves.

It is important for each and everyone to understand that they are responsible for their own actions. There can be no putting the blame on authority or peers. Each one should learn right and wrong and how to apply these principles in real circumstances. There is no lazy way out where we elect a politician to decide right and wrong for us. The politician is there to represent what we consider to be right or wrong.

All of us must become aware of the fact that we have such latent tendencies that can arise under certain conditions. Then we must develop the self-control that will enable us to defy and overcome these tendencies should they arise.

This is analogous to being prepared for a terrorist attack. The true terrorist is hidden in our subconscious minds. We must purify our minds so that the latent tendencies are destroyed before they can rise up. We must develop our self-control under ordinary circumstances so that we can control ourselves when extraordinary circumstances arise.

Miracles Happen

One of the great *yogis* about whom many miraculous events can be historically verified is almost forgotten. He has been mentioned in the classic Autobiography of a Yogi by Yogananda. He was a friend of arguably the greatest yogi messiah of modern times, Lahiri Mahasaya, the Guru of Yogananda's Guru. However, he was more famous during their lives, since he was already over two hundred years old when they met and meditated together. In fact, it was his testimony to Lahiri's divine status that silenced many critics of the householder *yogi*. He was a giant of a man in body as well as spirit. He was popularly called Trailanga Swami, but was born Shivaram in 1601 in a village near Vizianagaram in Andhra Pradesh, and chose to leave his body in 1881.

Even as a child he was considered a divine being, but it was only when he was forty years, after the death of his mother, that he became a renunciate. After doing twelve years of *sadhana*, he met his Guru Bhagiratananda Saraswati and was initiated into the higher dimensions of Yoga. He was then given the name of Gajanan Saraswati, but he was called by ordinary folks as Trailanga Swami. He maintained silence or mauna for many years at a time and would move from place to place.

Once, the king of Nepal and his retinue were hunting a tiger which entered a cave where Trailanga Swami was meditating. When the king entered the cave, he saw that the tiger was sitting near the yogi, gentle as a cat, and did not fire his gun out of respect for a saint. Opening his eyes, Trailanga Swami assured the king that the tiger would not even growl at them and asked him to come nearer. The king was so impressed, he asked him to be his guest at the palace, but instead the yogi chose to stay at the Pashupatinath temple, the seat of Gorakhnath in Nepal. However, as the crowds kept coming to see him, he retired into the jungles and did not return.

Another time, he went to Varanasi, the abode of Lord Shiva. He was then weighing over three hundred pounds, even though he was seldom seen to eat, and then only infrequently drink milk. Trailanga Swami was a *digambara*, that is, he went around totally nude and oblivious to the societal concerns. An English magistrate saw him lying naked on the road, and had him tried and put into prison. But that very night, he was seen wandering around the roof and no one could figure out how he had gotten out of the locked cell. Another magistrate, disbelieving reports of such a saint, had the huge *yogi* locked up again and put his most trusted men to guard the cell. Inexplicably, the Trailanga Swami was found the next morning walking in the streets and the guards had no explanation.

A third English magistrate in Varanasi decided to put the yogi to a test and invited him to come to his court and asked him whether he truly saw God everywhere as he claimed. He then asked him to eat garbage collected by his men. The saint put his hand on the plate of garbage and everything turned into delicious Indian sweets and he ate them. After this display, the English stopped bothering him anymore.

Trailanga Swami spent over one hundred and fifty years in Varanasi, a great blessing for the people, since such saints seldom stayed in one place for long, and usually shunned the gathering of large groups of people. What his work was cannot be fathomed by shallow minds such as ours, but must have been of a stupendous nature. The miracles attributed to him would be only a shadow of this true greatness. Many people have attested to seeing him floating in the Ganges river for days and weeks at a time, oblivious to events around him.

To show a lesson in detachment, he went on a boat with the grand king of the area. The king had come with his full finery in honor of the saint and was carrying his ceremonial golden sword with diamond studded sheath. It was a priceless heirloom. When he showed it to the saint, Trailanga Swami promptly threw it into the river. The king was crestfallen, but the laughing saint put his hand into the river and came up with five similar swords. The king could not tell which was his. This incident reduced his pride and attachment to objects.

It is said that in 1869, a young man called Ramakrishna who would later become a great *yogi* and saint came to Varanasi to get the blessing of Trailanga Swami. To teach the true nature of things, Trailanga Swami took his urine and poured it on the image of the Goddess worshipped by Ramakrishna, and asked him whether there was any difference between his urine and the holy water of the Ganges. Of this experience, Paramahansa Ramakrishna would say that he saw the Universal Lord Himself using the body of the saint as a vehicle for His manifestation.

The Divine comes and goes. Sometimes it is made obvious to even the most obtuse of us, and other times, great discrimination is needed to have the awareness. We must always be on the lookout and pray that we will have the grace and good *karma* to meet and recognize the Divine.

Homage to Yogananda

By the grace of Shiva-Goraksha-Babaji, Mukunda Lal Ghosh was born in the northern Indian town of Gorakhpur on January 5ᵗʰ, 1893. Gorakhpur is one of the main centers dedicated to the worship of the Mahavatar Babaji who has guided the spiritual evolution of humanity for eons. Mukunda was to later become the world renowned yogi, Parmahansa Yogananda, whose life-work was to introduce true spirituality to the West. He was the bridge between the East and the West.

Although widely respected and venerated, his true work is still not fully recognized. The immensity of what he achieved in his lifetime may never be truly known. His skillful means of transmitting alien concepts and difficult practices through innovative methods that had not been used before is unprecedented. His influence on many spiritual movements in the West is unheralded.

We can only pay our humble homage to such a selfless Master in the silence of our hearts, in the bliss of our meditations, and in the roar of Om.

Born into a devout and well-to-do Bengali family, Yogananda was encouraged to pursue his own spiritual path at an early age. By age 11, he was having mystical experiences, and, in one such episode in 1904, his mother, who was traveling away from home at the time, appeared to him in a vision. The vision informed him of her imminent death before anyone else in the home even knew that she was ill, and she died just as he had foreseen. His mother had left him a message prior to her death, informing him of his destiny and leaving him an amulet, which opened him to the guidance of teachers from past lives.

Yogananda was then impelled to visit sages and saints, even fleeing home and school occasionally, in a burning desire to find his Guru whose face had appeared to him in a vision. His quest finally led him to Swami Sri Yukteswar, the pre-eminent Master of Kriya Yoga, in 1910, and, for the next ten years, he studied under this master's loving discipline. After graduating from Calcutta University in July 1915, he vowed to devote his life to the love and service of God. He received the name Yogananda, meaning bliss (ananda) through union with the Divine (yoga) when he was initiated into the monastic Swami Order, by his Guru.

Thus began his tireless work to promulgate the teachings of the deathless Babaji, who had initiated Lahiri Mahasaya into Kriya Yoga. In turn Lahiri Mahasaya had passed on his teachings to others, including Sri Yukteswar. One of the distinctive marks of Kriya Yoga was that it was well-suited to the life-style of a householder, and brought the goal of Self-realization within the reach of the ordinary person with a family and responsibilities. The myth that only by renouncing one's family could a spiritual seeker attain to final liberation had been exploded by these Kriya Masters, who were all families and lived their lives in awareness and God-attunement without sacrificing their responsibilities. These spiritual giants discharged their duties without attachment.

In 1917, Yogananda founded a school for boys that combined yoga training and spiritual instruction with modern educational methods. He joked in his autobiography that, having renounced family life, he became father to more boys than he ever would otherwise have had.

A pivotal point came, when Babaji instructed Sri Yukteswar to prepare Yogananda for the great task for which he'd been born, the spiritualization of the Western World. In 1920, Yogananda was appointed to be one of the international delegates to a congress of religious leaders to be held in Boston. He knew nobody in the United States, and nobody knew anything of him. But that would change rapidly.

Yoganandaji's maiden address in Boston, on **"The Science of Religion,"** exploring the common threads between the world's religions, was enthusiastically received. For the next several years, he lectured and taught on the East coast of the United States, and in 1924 he embarked on a cross-continental speaking tour. He started a two-month series of lectures and classes in Los Angeles in January of 1925.

As elsewhere, his talks were greeted with interest and acclaim. The Los Angeles Times reported: "The Philharmonic Auditorium presents the extraordinary spectacle of thousands…being turned away an hour before the advertised opening of a lecture with the 3000-seat hall filled to its utmost capacity."

During the next decade his work and spirit brought him many famous students, including Luther Burbank, George Eastman, and Leopold Stokowski. In 1927, Paramahansa Yogananda was invited to meet President Calvin Coolidge at the White House. In less than a century, he would be hailed as the father of yoga in the West for his pioneering role in making known India's ancient philosophy of yoga and its time-honored tradition of meditation.

Yogananda's arrival in America from India initiated an upsurge of interest in the spiritual wisdom of the East. Through his life and teachings, he made an indelible impression on the spiritual landscape of the United States and the world. "Yogananda has become an image — a remarkable, deep, sweet, poetic, ecstatic man enraptured of cosmic life — who has changed the map of American religious life," writes Robert S. Ellwood, Ph.D., the former chairman of University of Southern California's School of Religion.

This "Hindoo Holy Man" as the headlines of day called him, has great influence to this day though his best-selling life story, the classic **Autobiography of a Yogi**, which was published in 1946 and expanded by him in subsequent editions. In 1999 the book was named one of the one hundred most influential spiritual books of the twentieth century. Phyllis Tickle, a contributing editor to *Publishers Weekly* noted, "Few books … have had greater impact on popular theology than Paramahansa Yogananda's *Autobiography of a Yogi.*" In *A New Religious America,* noted Harvard University Professor of Comparative Religions Diana Eck writes, "Yogananda put yoga on the map in America."

He stayed in the United States for the better part of three decades, introducing the principles of yoga and the art of balanced spiritual living to hundreds of thousands of people through his extensive public lecture tours, his numerous writings, and the centers he founded in the United States, Canada, and abroad.

In 1935, Yogananda began an 18-month tour of Europe and India during which he met statesmen, scientists, and spiritual figures. That year, his guru, Sri Yukteswar, bestowed on him the title Paramhansa[1] (meaning "supreme swan") recognizing his role as a World Teacher and great Soul.

India's great political and moral leader, Mahatma Gandhi invited Yogananda to his Wardha ashram. At Gandhiji's request he initiated the Mahatma and a few satyagrahis into the liberating technique of Kriya Yoga.

At about 7:00 PM on March 9, 1936, Yogananda's beloved guru, consciously entered into a supreme God communion state and through off his mortal coils. A few months later, on June 19, while Yoganandaji was meditating, a beautiful light appeared before him. It was Sri Yukteswar in his resurrected body to reveal through speech as well as through thought transference the laws of the universe and other esoteric matters. It is interesting to note that an image of Sri Yukteswar can be found on the cover art of the Beatles widely acclaimed "Sgt. Pepper's Lonely Heart's Club Band" album!

Yogananda's own physical death came on March 7, 1952, a conscious exit made after a speech given at a banquet. Twenty days later, according to a signed and notarized statement from the director of Forest Lawn Memorial Park, "no physical disintegration was visited upon his body...it was apparently in a phenomenal state of immutability." Yogananda's passing received widespread coverage in the press, including *The New York Times,* the *Los Angeles Times,* and *Time* magazine. In 1977, on the occasion of the 25th anniversary of Yogananda's passing, the government of India formally recognized his outstanding contributions to the spiritual upliftment of humanity by issuing a commemorative stamp in his honor, together with a tribute that read, in part:

"The ideal of love for God and service to humanity found full expression in the life of Paramahansa Yogananda. ... Though the major part of his life was spent outside India, still, [he] takes his place among our great saints. His work continues to grow and shine ever more brightly, drawing people everywhere on the path of the pilgrimage of the Spirit."

Yogananda's best-known written works include his **Autobiography of a Yogi**, published in 1946. Since its initial release, this book has been in continuous publication and translated into 18 languages. Through his writings he has been able to disseminate to a wide international audience his belief in the unity of the world's religions and to teach his methods for attaining direct personal experience of God. To serious students he taught Kriya yoga, a spiritual science including soul-awakening techniques that had been lost in the Dark Ages but revived by his Guru lineage.

Yogananda took every opportunity to foster interfaith understanding, brotherhood, and world peace. Just a sampling of his myriad efforts in this area include: speaking at a World Peace Meeting in Boston, 1922; speaking at a conference on interracial relations in New York, 1929; addressing the World Fellowship of Faiths at the Chicago World's Fair, 1933; speaking at the British National Council of World Fellowship of Faiths at Whitefields Institute in England, 1936; hosting an International Peace Program in Los Angeles, 1939; and addressing an international peace conference (which he helped organize) held in San Francisco during the inaugural meetings of the United Nations, 1945. "If we had a man like Paramahansa Yogananda in the United Nations today," said Dr. Binay R. Sen, former Indian ambassador to the United States, "probably the world would be a better place than it is."

In this new millennium, Yogananda's message is still relevant and just as needed. Global events continue to challenge people throughout the world to look at life from a deeper spiritual perspective, to seek a sense of inner peace and security that can withstand the changing winds of outer circumstances, and to discover the shared values that unify humanity, while acknowledging cultural and religious diversity. The core of Yogananda's mission addressed these very concerns, and his spiritual teachings provide answers as relevant to seekers today as when he began his mission more than eighty-six years ago.

The core of Yogananda's work involved Kriya Yoga. Although the actual practice of Kriya Yoga is not given in books to the public to ensure its proper and beneficial transmission, his whole life, speeches and writings give the Essence of Kriya Yoga.

In the Light of Kriya

In light of Kriya absorbed
Reflections five, single appeared
Accumulated effects indeed
Of thoughts, words and deeds.

No perfect strangers are these
Sense desire, attachment born
Elements, ignorant body form
Manifestations of *karmic* bonds.

Ever vigilant guide residing
Heart's light by Guru's grace
Mine Eye in *dharma* abiding
Marvel at maya's magic maze.

Once sunk in sensory festivity
Embracing illusion's reality
Lost in dreams's finality
Web of time, space, causality.

Fourfold *dharma* creates and upholds
Visible and invisible cosmic laws
Tiniest quark to mightiest quasar unfolds
Human chaos, inherent nature rules.

Justice *karma* engine drives
Impersonal wheel - life and death
Three-fold *karma* slave's drama
Past actions present birth create.

In awe, a glimpse of universal law
Soul imprints for propriety
Right or wrong puzzle jigsaw
Moral imperatives save society.

In Light of Kriya Yoga

Nature tendencies and in-born aptitudes
Race and physical characteristics
Family, friends and social attitudes
Genes and stars give the show away.

Good news yogic sages describe
Birth death vicious cycle depart
A three-fold remedy describe
Liberation ,bliss eternal impart.

Non-attachment actions fruit deny
Life's acceptance righteous living
Sincere sadhana unripe seeds burn
Be ever-constant in selfless giving.

A thousand lifetimes' tears defeat
Heart's soul cry for divine guide
Complete surrender upon lotus feet
Heart's temple door open wide.

Golden-hued youth shows the way
Across suffering ocean's sway
Straight away to undying light
Right away from fog of night.

Grace born of illuminating ray
Transcending limited life's stay
Gift of blessed *sadhana* way
Skillful means hasten light and day

Rhythmic breath bind restless mind
Hamsa *mantra* true Self to find
Karmic motion by *dharma* bind
Alchemy's complete gift: no-mind.

Patanjali sage in sutras brief
Eightfold kriya path pronounced
Yama, self-restraint is the ground
Self-control first stage announced

Aspiring yogi, *yama* practice must
Steer actions to liberation's sight
Niyama too for karmic merit trust
Turn future tide to clear light.

Austere sacrifice, fire and heat
Babaji's kriya persevere
Burns slag of past evil *karmas*
Exposes Soul's golden splendor.

By spinal breathing true
Superconsciousness arise
Removes causlity's glue
As ego-mine in fire dies.

In light of kriya absorbed
Kundalini ego-sting
Triple knots dissolved
Om, shiva-shakti ring.

Constant Self-study - who am I?
Illusion body-mind, true Spirit
See star-self in third-eye
Body-mind only by union lit.

From ego-magnet desires lies
Will roast in wisdom's fires
Like-dislike attraction relate
Karma seeds cannot germinate.

In Light of Kriya Yoga

Heed God Essence within
Seek harmony in contentment
Complete surrender no sin
Let go personal attachment.

Christ Jesus taught all to pray
May Lord's will be done in us
Free choice God's will obey
In *dharma* deed, no pain no fuss.

In unconditioned *samadhi* bliss
No *dharma* nor *karma* knows
The Self-realized Yogiraj glows
Life and livingness shows.

Only spiritual crutches these he knows
A slave's redemption for ego-souls
Though if truth eternal be told
No path or transformation spirit knows.

Pluck out sufferings causal root
Knowledge gives ignorance the boot
Know now everything as Self
Not even an atom as other.

Reality's wisdom realized
Action reaction, limit no more
Sense elements, duality resolved
Dreamer awakes to dream no more.

In the light of kriya absorbed
Bhakti love and shakti might
Time, space, causality dissolved
Om, Great Swan takes flight.

Liberation

Moksha
Free from death
Free from birth
Free from rebirth
Free from sorrow
Free from *karma*
Free from desire
Free from ignorance
Free from the finite
Free from evil
Being Pure
Being Self-Realized
Being Divine
Being Immortal
Being Perfect
Being Enlightened

Over two thousand five hundred years ago, a young prince named Siddhartha became disillusioned with life and decided to seek liberation from old age, sickness and death. He became the great yogi called the Buddha. Liberation or *moksha* has twin aspects like two sides of a coin – one aspect is the quest for freedom from all suffering, while the other is the attainment of the Self-Realization or the wisdom of immortality.

Both aspects are exemplified in the follow words of the sage of the Chandogya Upanishad (7.26.2), the first aspect is in the first two verses while the second aspect in the third and fourth verses:

The seer sees not death,
Nor sickness nor any distress.
The seer sees only the All,
Obtains the All entirely.

Although it is the suffering of life that generally spurs one onto the spiritual path, the yogis tell us that only by seeking the True Self is there freedom from the cycle of life and death:

> *By knowing God, there is a falling off of all chains,*
> *with distresses destroyed; there is a cessation of birth and*
> *death.*
> Svestasvatara Upanishad 1.11

In ancient times, by the banks of a holy river lived a great sage called Maharishi Sumedhasa. He was renowned throughout the land for his divine wisdom and many lost souls came to his ashram for refuge.

During those days, a king called Suratha had lost his kingdom to his enemies after being betrayed by his ministers. He only just retained his life by riding his swift horse into the forest. He became a wanderer. At the same time, in another part of India, the wealthiest merchant of the land called Samadhi had been betrayed by his greedy family members and lost all his riches, houses and lands. He also became wanderer. Both these men came to the ashram of Sumedhasa for protection and was given permission by the sage to stay.

However, even though they were in the midst of wise men, they were always unhappy and their minds were filled with sorrow and agony for what they had lost. They were still in bondage to the illusion of life, to the attachments to possessions and to family and friends.

They sought out the sage and begged for release from suffering, liberation from their agony.

Sumedhasa then initiated them into the spiritual path and gave them a mantra of the Divine Mother, who is both the cause and liberation from Maya or illusion.

The two men then sat down on the river bank and started their practice. For four years they meditated. In the first year they ate only fruit which had fallen to the ground. The second year, they ate only fallen leaves and the third year they existed only on *prana* or life-force.

Finally the Divine Mother came and blessed them for their strong spiritual practice. She told them she would grant them whatever they asked of Her.

The former king still had some ignorance left and requested that he would get back his kingdom and be reborn in his next life as an Emperor of the world. She smiled and granted his request.

On the other hand, the former merchant was lost in the bliss of the Mother's vision and all he asked for was liberation. He was taken onto the Mother's lap and attained to liberation or *moksha*.

> *He obtains all worlds and all desires who has found out*
> *and who understands the True Self.*
> *Chandhogya Upanishad 8.7.1*

That is Perfect
This is perfect
From that Perfection comes
this perfection
The waves of perfection arise in the
Ocean of Perfection
Yet that Perfection is never lost.
May there be peace in this world
May there be peace in the subtle realms
May there be peace in the beyond

- interpretation of verse 1 from Ishapanishad

Herbs and Yoga

Yogis have always been known as experts in the utilization of natural herbs for the prevention or curing of diseases, as well as for enhancing the yogic practices of their students. Agastya, the great Himalayan *rishi* who developed South Indian culture is also credited with instituting the *Siddha* science of herbs. The perfected *yogis* called variously *Naths* and *Siddhas* also originated the branch of *Ayurveda* (the ancient *Vedic* science of health and healing) called *rasayana* or path of longevity that included the practices called *kaya kalpa* or physical and mental rejuvenation. It is interesting to note that the *Vedic* science of medicine also uses *yogic* tools, such as *asanas* (physical postures), *pranayama* (breathing techniques), *mantras* (audible formulae of energy and power) and meditation as part of their system of healing. There is a close inter-relationship between Yoga and *Ayurveda*.

According to Patanjali, a great *siddha* and author of the Yoga Sutras, herbs are legitimate tools for becoming a *siddha* or perfected yogi:

> *The accomplishments (of perfection in Yoga) are the results of birth, herbs, mantras, intense practice and cognitive absorption.*

Yoga Sutras IV.1

In more modern times, it was mentioned in Yogananda's spiritual masterpiece, "Autobiography of a Yogi," that Panchanon Battacharya, a Kriya Master and disciple of Lahiri Mahasaya, set-up a mission in Calcutta to teach Kriya Yoga and give herbal remedies.

Following Patanjali, it is important to note that herbs do not replace the other tools and factors, such as intense practice, for success in the path of Self-Realization. Additionally, these herbs are generally taken in conjunction with a healthy diet – it would be counterproductive to feed the body all the poisons of processed foods and meats from our mineral-depleted and junk-food culture, and hope for the positive effects of these transformational herbs. A healthy life-style without dependencies on habit-forming drugs and intoxicants, sufficient rest and sleep, are pre-requisites for a strong spiritual practice that can benefit from the use of herbs.

Some of the yogic masters were also alchemists and they used metals and other chemicals to help in the transformation of the body and mind. However, such practices are extremely dangerous and impossible to implement without the guidance of an experienced teacher, of which there are hardly any in contemporary society, notwithstanding some claims to the contrary.

On the other hand, there are many herbs that have been used for millennia, with well-understood and documented effects. Many are also now widely available in *Ayurvedic* stores or on the Internet. Of the hundreds of herbs, there are especially five that can be considered by all practitioners of Yoga. They are *shanka pushpi, ashwagandha, brahmi, guggulu* and *shatavari*. They help in two ways, first by increasing the physical and mental immunity to diseases – if one is struck down by illness, then it is difficult to meditate. Secondly, they help to increase the capacity of the body and mind to be transformed by the yogic techniques.

The following is a brief introduction to the benefits of these five yogic herbs:

Shanka Pushpi:
This is for rejuvenation of the mind. It improves memory and concentration, and stimulates the development of creativity centers in the brain.

Ashwagandha:
Often called the Indian Ginseng, it is the best healing herb for both body and mind. Physically, it strengthens the nervous and skeletal

systems, that is the nerves, bones, tendons and muscles, relieving aches and pains in joints. For the mind, it is calming and can reduce anxiety and insomnia, promoting concentration and deep sleep. This is an excellent herb to aid in both the physical endurance and mental alertness required of long spiritual practices.

Brahmi:
As the name suggests, this herb is used to gain knowledge of the Divine Creator. It helps to control anger and attachments, by calming the mind. It also stimulates certain parts of the brain to configure it for higher consciousness.

Guggulu:
This is an excellent herb for longevity. It promotes flexibility of the muscles, ligments and bones for a steady and pain free posture. It also lowers cholesterol and strengthens the heart. It is a blood cleanser and also regulates blood sugar.

Shatavari

This is a good general tonic but specifically for countering fever, acidity and dehydration. It calms the heart and increases love and devotion.

These herbs are available in powder form, in capsules, or made into tinctures or even jams (often in combination with other herbs). It is easiest to take them in capsules or pills. If taken in powder form, then generally there will be directions to mix it with warm milk, honey or some other way, as they all are rather "untasty" for the normal palate.

Different physiologies will react differently to these herbs due to the human range of sensitivity. Each person will need to take responsibility for the use of these potent herbs. It is best to start out with a strengthening regime of *shanka pushpi* and *ashwagandha* for at least two weeks, before adding *brahmi* for another week, followed by a week of *guggulu*, and finally *shatavari*.

If the benefits are observed, without any undesirable side-effects, then a daily regimen of all five herbs should be taken for optimum effect. They will have a strengthening effect on all five bodies, the physical, energetic, emotional, mental and causal.

note: there is a misunderstanding among spiritual visitors to India who notice that some sadhus ustilize marijuana and other strong drugs, that it implies approval for their use. This is incorrect. Since ancient times, certain herbs have been used to withstand the rigors of the Himalayan cold. Yogis spend their nights in freezing caves or in the open. Sometimes they have to walk with no food for many miles in rugged terrain. This is seldom the case for modern yogis. In special cases, Masters have been known to prescribe specific mind-altering and / or enhancing herbs, but only for removing certain blockages - not for general consumption. Drugs are an impediment on the spiritual path.

Leading A Spiritual Life In A Material World

Kriya Yoga teaches that one should make progress and achieve Self-Realization while acting as a householder. This requires not just an outward renunciation of the world, nor the actual retiring to a cave, but an inner renunciation, a non-attachment to the material world. It requires that the *kriya* initiate skillfully lives and works in the world of impermanence and ultimate illusion, deriving the resources necessary to accomplish the spiritual goal of achieving the experience of reality.

An example often cited by the ancient yogis is that of the lotus plant that grows and flowers in the muddy waste-waters, but is not tainted by its surroundings. It remains pure, while absorbing the nutrients from the water and the sun.

In the Bhagavad-Gita, Lord Krishna counsels that we should offer the fruits of our actions to the Divine. In this way, we do not become enmeshed in the results of our actions and are free to do our best without attachment. To expect a reward from our actions is a material way of thinking, while to act selflessly without expectations is the spiritual way of being. Even when we are being paid for our services, we need not be attached to the money, but can offer it to the Divine, to be used to maintain our spiritual life and to help others.

Now, from a practical perspective, how should a spiritually inclined person act?

The first key to the spiritual life is to set-up and maintain a regular practice or *sadhana*. Regularity is critical in overcoming inertia and other obstacles to spiritual evolution. A daily practice, preferably once in the morning and once in the evening, no matter how brief, is superior to intermittent efforts performed for hours. This is due to the continual accumulation of negativity that must be overcome before they have the opportunity to take root in the subconscious.

Once rooted and supported by existing negative habit patterns, then the effort to eradicate them become ten times more difficult.

Even in mundane matters, we have learnt to brush our teeth everyday – waiting every three days and then brushing for half an hour would seem absurd to our sensibilities. There are those who would brush their teeth after every meal to prevent the build-up of plaque. Take this same enthusiasm into your spiritual life. Perform your *sadhana* regularly and prevent the build-up of negativity and *karma*.

The second key is to maintain a constant awareness of our spiritual goal. This awareness is often disrupted by our uneven and irregular life-style. Therefore, it is necessary to examine one's life-style. Take a few moments to note down your daily and weekly activities and examine them. Do you take enough rest, or are you depriving yourself of your health by insufficient sleep? Are you eating healthy food, deriving sufficient life-force or *prana* to remain energetic and positive? It is paradoxical that taking good care of the material body is a mark of spirituality. This does not mean that one should fall into the trap of compulsive dieting, exercising, or absorption in body beautification procedures, which have become part of our consumer culture. However, a consistent asana or postures practice is highly beneficial for the physical and energy bodies.

A healthy body is necessary for spiritual evolution. It is recorded that the great *yogi* Siddhartha Gautama mortified his body through excessive fasting and found that he could not make any further progress in his meditation. Finally, he was so weak that he was dying, rather than evolving, and so he crawled to a stream and bathed himself, ate a small meal, rested and continued his meditation, subsequently achieving enlightenment, becoming the Buddha. He always taught moderation in all things – the middle way.

The third key is to find a balance between spiritual and material activities. How much time do you devote to your spiritual life? It is not necessary to spend all your time or even the majority of your time on spiritual activities. However, examine your material activities and determine their necessity. Doing things with your family is necessary and working is necessary to support oneself and one's family. Is working late and taking work home necessary? Is watching television necessary? What is commonly called entertainment is usually an excuse for stimulating a tired mind. Rest and meditation may be a better remedy. Strike a balance.

The fourth key is to examine the people we associate with - the relationships that we value. This does not mean that one should give up our long-cherished friendships because they do not involve spiritual activities. It is helpful to cultivate friends who share similar spiritual aspirations and who can provide much needed support. There is a tendency among those new to the spiritual path to try to explain their new beliefs and practices or even attempt to convince close friends to join them. This should be done very delicately and not from a missionary perspective. If one finds that they are not receptive, one should stop annoying them. It is never productive to force your beliefs on others. To keep their friendship, you would need to downplay your spiritual activities. If and when they wish to know more, they will know to ask you. Don't expect understanding and support from even close family members. They fear the unknown and they fear to lose you. Have patience to explain what you are doing – you may have to explain many times, until they see that you are not becoming a fanatic or ignoring them.

The fifth key is to examine one's work. Since most of us spend the majority of our day at work, if its performance is a hindrance to our spiritual values, then we need to consider a change. It is possible to work and have provision for financial sustenance without compromising ourselves, or selling our integrity. It is needful to keep in mind the values of truth (*satya*), non-harming of ourselves and others (*ahimsa*) and non-stealing (*asteya*), when examining our work. Another value to keep in mind is our self-actualization – is the work that you are doing utilizing your highest potential? Are you happy in this type of work, or did you stumble or got driven into it? Is this what you want in your life? Consider moving from a high paying but unsatisfying role to a more satisfying position, or moving from a dull low paying job to becoming self-employed.

The possibilities are many, but we need to have confidence in the Divine will. We need to tune in to the Divine and find our *dharma* or right path in this world. When we came into this world, we came with the self-imposed burden of *karma*, but also with the promise of the right path or *dharma* for all of us. By following our *dharma*, we can overcome all our *karma*, and achieve Self-Realization in this life.

Constant awareness of our goal and constant vigilance of our activities will help us steer a spiritual path through the turbulent seas of materiality.

It is a blessing to know that we need and not be enmeshed in what we want. It is a blessing to be satisfied with what we have and not desire what we don't need.

Joyful Living

We all seek to lead a happier life. No one, not even the most powerful person, nor the wealthiest person can honestly say that they cannot be happier. Only the sage and *yogi* have no desire for greater happiness. Such a one lives in joy, for they have realized that they have come from bliss and have now returned to bliss. What about the rest of us, the one's struggling in some intermediate state? In their compassion, those who have experienced reality have given certain guideline that everyone can follow in order to increase their level of happiness.

The sages have taught that there are four primary motives in every life:
- Dharma: the path of justice and truth
- Artha: the path of work and wealth
- Kama: the path of sensual satisfaction
- Moksha: the path of liberation

All of us have aspects of all four motives in our lives, but one or the other will be the primary goal of one life – the path we were born to follow. Then there is the actual path that we are following - this may change as we pass through different phases and responsibilities. When we are young we may be motivated by the path of wealth and sensual desires, but as we grow older, we may think more and more about *moksha*.

Joy comes from recognizing the appropriate life-path for any particular phase of life and following that path. Unhappiness comes from ignoring your right path. A person who has taken up the responsibilities of a family must tread the path of *artha* or risk starving his family. It is not appropriate to take off to the caves and leave one's family – this would be against *dharma*. Even if that person was born to follow the path of liberation, this may have to be done in tandem with the path of work and wealth, as a householder *yogi*.

231

All of us have to act. No one can stop themselves from affecting the world in some way or the other. We normally act from desire and we evaluate the results of our actions from the viewpoint of whether it satisfies our initial desire. If the results are not satisfactory, then unhappiness arises. Most of the time, the results are only partially satisfactory and so there is mixed happiness and disappointment. Even when the results exceed our expectations the happiness that arises is brief, as our mind has gone on to evaluating the next action.

Ego-centric action cannot give lasting joy. The sages recommend selfless action without any personal expectations. Joy comes from dedicating our actions to the Divine and acting to our best abilities for the benefit of all beings without expecting or taking any credit for the results.

In spite of our best intentions, we often commit actions which produce negative impact on ourselves or others – we can control our own actions but we cannot predict the results. Therefore to take credit for positive results will require us to take the consequences of the negative results and we continue on the roller-coaster of *karma*. By the sincere dedication of our actions to the Divine we stop the cycle of regret and despair and start to tread the path of joy.

The sages have recommended the virtue of surrendering to the Divine as a recipe for a joyful life. Surrender is not a word that normally has a positive ring to it. We're not taught by family or society to value surrender. It is better to win then lose – we're taught never to give up. So how can we resolve this material need to win with the often heard and repeated, but seldom practiced advice to surrender spiritually?

A great sage Patanjali has given "total surrender to the Divine" as the most important part of the definition for the science of Self-Realization. What are we to give up? It is our negativity. This may seem like it should be very easy, since no one should want to keep their negativities. However, this actually flies in the face of reality. In our day-to-day experiences, we see people holding on to their angers, fears, hatred and desires, rather than giving them up. We see daily the venting of frustrations in road-rage and discourtesies perceived in public areas, and privately with family and friends. There are those who advise the expression of one's negative emotions, rather than holding them back! Now, if we keep in our frustrations, we run the risk of psychosomatic illnesses, but if we give vent to our rage, then we can harm others. There is a third option, which is to give them up to the Divine, releasing them back to the Source of all.

Now, if it seems that we can be reluctant to give up our faulty habits, imagine how we might feel about surrendering our hard-earned virtues. In order to achieve higher states of consciousness, we are advised by the yogis to surrender our good works, achievements and positive habits as well, to the Divine. If we hold back anything, we cannot achieve perfect attunement with the Goddessence.

There is an instructive story to illustrate the surrender of even our dearest wishes and achievements to Divine:

The Lord of Yoga came down from the lofty heights in the Himalayas, together with his partner Parvati, to visit with the advanced yogis. The Lord was there to check on their spiritual progress, to give helpful pointers and encouragement to those striving for Self-Realization.

At one hermitage, there were a number of very powerful yogis who practiced day and night. One old servant dutifully took care of their needs. Since the old servant was not able to practice any advanced techniques, all he did was to repeat the name of the Lord and he was content.

While Lord Shiva was visiting them, each yogi came to him and asked Him about their progress and how much longer they must practice before enlightenment. To all of them He would praise them for their efforts, and to one, he would say, three more lives,

*to a second, two more lives and to a third, one more life ... however,
all the yogis felt unhappy and wished that they could achieve
liberation in that life-time. They kept quiet but their minds were
disturbed even though they only had one desire left- that of
liberation, but they had not surrendered it to the Divine.*

*At last when the Lord was leaving, the old servant humbly
approached Him and also asked about his own progress. The Lord
saw that it would take another thousand lives before the old man
would achieve Self-Realization, but did not want to discourage
him, and only said, "My son, you are making good progress, and
sooner or later, you will be with me."*

*The old man then began to dance about, repeating the Lord's name
and giving thanks. No sooner did he did do this, that the old man
suddenly become young and was transported to the abode of the
Lord in a blaze of light.*

*Parvati was puzzled and asked Lord Shiva what had happened.
The Lord then responded that the old man had given up all
attachments, even that for liberation, and was totally single-
heartedly surrendered to the Divine, and by trusting totally in His
words, was instantly transformed.*

Such is the power of devotion and total surrender. Even before Self-
Realization, a joyful life is realized by the surrender of our desires to
the Lord.

We can even strive to surrender our very breath to the Divine, to realize
that it is the Divine who is breathing through us. Even if we forget to
think of God our whole lives, it would not be a problem for God, but if
even for an instant the Divine forgot about us, we would instantly blink
out of existence.

.

In order to know our path in life, to act without attachment and to surrender ourselves to the Divine, we must develop constant awareness and an inner purity to burn away all negativities. It is the actualization of Jesus' injunction in the Lord's Prayer: "Your will be done on earth, as it is in heaven," uniting the macrocosmic to the microcosmic, the Divine with the human soul.

Living with awareness is living in joy. It is the awareness that arises when we are watching an engrossing movie and still know that it is a movie. When we lose our awareness we become trapped in our self-made delusions. Joy comes from seeing through the illusions of the world and the ego created delusions of what will make us happy.

Let go of our delusions of finitude. Embrace life. Live life large. In whatever path you are pursuing, make space for the Divine. From the ego flows only suffering. Only from the Divine flows joy

Live God

No one is ever alone
God is always with us
God is always in us
See God, Hear God
Taste God, Smell God
Feel God – everywhere
At night in bed, as we sleep
God holds our hands
Every breath – God breathes
Through us and in us
God will never forsake us
In the dark, God is light
God is the light in the heart
Put aside the mind
Hear the pure heart
Resounding amen find
God is within and without
Turn towards God
Follow your inner voice
God speaks to you
God speaks through you
Life is precious
No time for depression
No time for grief
No time for anger
Time only for
Love, light and joy
Forgive all your hurts
Forsake all your desires
God loves you
Love God, Live God

Rudra Shivananda

Every End carries a new Beginning
Just as every Beginning has to End

Glossary

A

Adharma. A lack of virtue or righteousness

Adrishta. The impelling, unseen power of one's own past actions

Agni. The cosmic Fire element

Ahamkara. The 'I-maker' - the individuation principle, or ego, which must be transcended for Self-realization

Ahimsa. Non-harming – an important moral discipline (*yama*)

Ajna Chakra. Third-eye; sixth energy center, in the center of the head

Akasha. Ether/space - the first of the five material elements of which the physical universe is composed

Anahata Chakra. Heart center; the fifth energy center

Ananda. Bliss - the state of utter joy, which is an essential quality of the ultimate Reality

Apana. Aspect of life-force energy in the body, functioning in excretion

Apas. The cosmic Water element

Asana. Seat - a physical posture; originally this meant only a meditation posture, but has subsequently been greatly developed in Hatha Yoga

Ashtanga. The eight-limbed comprehensive yogic system

Atman. Self - the true Self, or Spirit, which is eternal and super-conscious

Avatar. A divine incarnation, such as Rama, Krishna from Vishnu, and Babaji from Shiva

Avidya. Ignorance - the root cause of suffering (*duhkha*)

B

Babaji. Immortal being responsible for the spiritual evolution of mankind. He works in the background, without interfering with the free-will of humanity. See also *Gorakshanath. Babaji* is the
Ancient of Days. He was first brought to the notice of the West in *Yogananda's* classic, 'Autobiography of a Yogi'

Bandha. A physical lock in yogic postures

Bhakta. Devotee - a disciple practicing *Bhakti-Yoga*

Bhakti. Devotion - the love of the devotee toward the Divine or the *guru*

Bhastrika. A type of purifying breath control exercise

Bhuta Shuddhi. Purification of the five elements which constitute the physical and subtle bodies

Bija. A seed or source

Brahma. The Divine principle of Creation; Creator of the universe

Brahmacharya. The discipline of chastity, which produces *ojas*

Buddha. The 'awakened one' - designation of the person who has attained enlightenment; title of *Gautama*, the historic founder of Buddhism, who lived in the sixth century B.C.E.

Buddhi. Intellect; understanding, reason; light of consciousness

C

Chakra. Wheel - one of the psycho-energetic centers of the subtle body
Cit. Consciousness; the super-conscious ultimate Reality
Chitta. Mind-stuff; mental substratum

D

Deva. The shining one - a male deity or a high angelic being
Devi. She who shines - a female deity or a high angelic being
Dharma. Law – right conduct
Dhyana. Meditation
Diksha. A transfer of wisdom or power through initiation
Dosha. A fault; the categories of physical constitution in the medical system of *Ayurveda*

G

Goraksha. Lord of the senses ['protector of cows'] - the Immortal founder of *Hatha-Yoga*; disciple of *Matsyendranath*. See also *Gorakshanath* and *Babaji*
Gorakshanath. The formal designation for *Goraksha*, as the founder of the *Nath Sampradaya*, the ancient upholders of *Yoga*
Guna. The fundamental building blocks of nature expressed as a triad of brightness, activity and inertia
Guru. A spiritual teacher; *acarya*; literally, "he who is heavy, weighty"

H

Hamsa. Swan – the Soul; particularly for that which is being propelled by the breath
Hatha-Yoga. A major branch of Yoga, developed by *Gorakshanath*; Ha-tha is the union of the sun and moon; with
 emphasis on the energetic and physical tools of transformation, such as postures, cleansing techniques, and breath control

I

Ida-nadi. The energy or *prâna* current on the left side of the central channel (*sushumna-nadi*) associated with the
 parasympathetic nervous system and having a cooling or calming effect on the mind when activated
Ishvara-pranidhana. Dedication to the Lord – surrender to the will of the Divine; one of the *Niyamas*, or *Ashtanga*

J
Japa. The recitation of *mantras*
Jivatman. The 'individual self' as opposed to the ultimate Self (*parama-âtman*)
Jivan-mukta. A Siddha who, while still embodied, has attained liberation (*moksha*)
Jnana. Knowledge/wisdom

K
Kaivalya. The state of absolute freedom from conditioned existence
Kama. Desire - the appetite for sensual pleasure blocking the path to true bliss (*ananda*)
Kapalabhati. A rapid breathing technique for purification of the energy body
Kapha. One of the doshas; predominance of Water element in the physical body constitution
Karma. Activity of any kind; the law of *karma* is the law of causation
Kevala kumbakha. Spontaneous cessation of breath
Khecari-mudra. The Hatha Yoga practice of curling the tongue back against the upper palate in order to seal the life energy (*prana*)
Kosha. Any one of five "envelopes" surrounding the true Self (*atman*) and thus blocking its light – the physical body is called *annamayakosha* ['envelope made of food']
Krishna. An incarnation of God Vishnu, the God-man whose teachings can be found in the *Bhagavad-Gita*
Kriya Yoga. An evolutionary practice for Self Realization, founded by Babaji
Kumbhaka. Breath retention; a part of *Pranayama*
Kundalini-shakti. The spiritual energy, which exists in potential form at the lowest psycho-energetic center of the body [*muladhara chakra*) and which must be awakened and guided to the center at the crown (*sahasrara chakra*) for Self Realization

M
Mahamudra. Great Seal. A practice of importance in Kriya Yoga
Manas. Mind - the lower mind, which is bound to the senses
Manipura chakra. The navel or third energy center
Mantra. A sacred sound or phrase, such as *om*, with a transforming effect on the mind of the individual reciting it; to be ultimately effective, a *mantra* needs to be given in an initiatory context (*dîkshâ*)
Matsyendranath. 'Lord of Fish' - Guru of Gorakshanath; a great Yogi, remembered by the Buddhists as Avalokiteshwara, the Boddhisatva of Compassion
Maya. Illusion by which the world is seen as separate from the ultimate Reality
Moksha. Release / Liberation - the condition of freedom from ignorance (*avidya*) and the binding effect of *karma*

N

Nadi. Energy Channel – there are 72,000 subtle channels through which the life force (*prana*) circulates

Nadi Shodana. Purification of the energy channels

Nadi Shuddhi. Purification of the energy channels

Nath. Lord – the Masters of Yoga

Nath Sampradaya. The tradition flowing through the mists of time, of the Lords of Yoga

Nauli. Abdominal churning exercise

Nirguna. The Eternal Reality beyond all qualities

Niyama. Self-restraint - the second limb of *Ashtanga*, which consists of purity (*shauca*), contentment (*samtosha*), austerity

(*tapas*), study (*svadhyaya*), and dedication to the Lord (*ishvara-pranidhana*)

O

Ojas. Vitality - the subtle spiritual energy produced from sexual energy through practice

Om — the original *mantra* symbolizing the ultimate Reality

P

Papa. Negative results caused by desire and ego-centeredness - eliminated when wisdom arises

Paramatman. Supreme self - the truel Self, which is one, as opposed to the plurality of individuated self (*jiva-atman*) existing in the form of living beings

Paramahamsa. Supreme swan – the state of a being, between liberation and Siddhahood

Pingala-nadi. The channel of the *prâna* or life-energy on the right side of the central channel (*sushumna-nadi*) and associated

with the sympathetic nervous system and having an energizing effect on the mind when activated

Pitta. One of the *doshas*; a dominance of the Fire element in the physical constitution

Prakriti. Nature, which is unconscious or *acit*

Prana. Life-force sustaining the body; the breath as an external manifestation of the subtle life-force

Pranayama. Breath control - from *prana* and *ayama* - life/breath extension")

Pratyahara. Internalization of the senses; the fifth limb in Ashtanga

Prithvi. The cosmic Earth element

Punya. Merit from righteous and moral action

Purakha. Inhalation phase of breathing

Purusha. The true Self (*atman*) or Spirit

R

Raja-Yoga. ("Royal Yoga") — a late medieval designation of *Patanjali's* eightfold *yoga-darshana,* also known as Classical Yoga, or Ashtanga

Rajas. One of the three Gunas; principle of activity and movement

Rama — an incarnation of God *Vishnu* preceding *Krishna*; the principal hero of the *Ramayana*

Rishi. Cosmic Seer – particularly apt for the Seven *Rishis*, who have ascended to the stars to help cosmic evolution

S

Sadhana. Spiritual discipline or practice leading to perfection

Saguna Brahman. The phenomenal aspect of the Divine

Sahaja. The *sahaja* state is the natural condition, that is, enlightenment or realization

Sahasrara Chakra. The crown or seventh energy center

Samadhi. The state of Yoga; the ecstatic unitive state; there are many types of *samadhi - samprajnâta* (with object), *asamprajnâta* (objectless) and *sahaja*(natural state of enlightenment)

Samsara. The finite world of change, as opposed to the ultimate Reality

Samskara. The subconscious impression left behind by each will-full act, which leads to habitual reactions

Sanatana Dharma. The Eternal Teachings of the sages and yogis

Sat. Being/truth - the ultimate Reality

Sat-Guru. The Guru of Truth – capable of giving the disciple the experience of super-consciousness

Satsang. Company of Truth – being in the company of a Master of Yoga

Sattva. One of the three *gunas*; the principle of light

Shakti. Energy - the dynamic aspect of the Divine; depicted as feminine

Shaktipat. Descent of energy – the transmission of spiritual energy from a Sat-Guru, to speed up the process of Self Realization in the disciple

Shambavi. A concentration technique with eyes, open and focused on the third-eye

Shishya. Student/disciple - the initiated disciple of a *guru*

Shiva. The Auspicious One – the supreme liberating aspect of the Divine; the supreme Yogi

Shuddhi. Purification

Siddha. Perfected Being

Surya. One of the names of our Sun, the highest visible manifestation of the Creative aspect of the Divine

Sushumna-nadi. The central *prâna* or life-force channel counterpart to the physical spinal cord; the *kundalini-shakti* ascends this channel during Self Realization

T

Tapas. Austerity; the fire, heat and light from *sadhana*

Tamas. One of the three *gunas*; the principle of inertia and ignorance

U

Udana. One of the aspect of the life-force energy

V

Vairagya. The abandonment of all passions

Vayu. Air; another term used for the aspects of *prana*

Vata. One of the *doshas*; a predominance of the Air element in the body

Vedanta. The primary non-dualistic metaphysical approach to reality based on the teachings of the Vedas and Upanishads

Vidya. Knowledge/wisdom

Vishnu. The preserver - the aspect of the Divine which has had in this cycle, nine incarnations, including *Rama* and *Krishna*; the tenth incarnation (*avatar*) *Kalki* is coming at the close of the *kali-yuga*

Vishuddha Chakra. The throat or fifth energy center

Viveka. Discernment or discriminating aspect of wisdom

Vritti. The waves of mental disturbance

Vyana. One of the aspects of the life-force energy; the *prana* which pervades the body

Y

Yajna. Sacrifice; Yoga is an inner sacrifice through meditation and self-surrender

Yoga. The state of Union with the Divine; the path of discipline and practice to achieve Self Realization

Yogi. A Self-Realized Being; commonly used also for a practitioner of Yoga, who has not yet achieved the goal

Note:
The following are a few of the many unique expressions often used by my Master Yogiraj Siddhanath in his lectures and books:
1. The Lightning Standing Still
2. The Alchemy of Total Transformation
3. The Lightless Light
4. Life and Livingness
5. The Ancient of Days
6. Shiva Goraksha Babaji
7. Shivapat

More Books by Rudra Shivananda

Chakra self-Healing by the Power of Om
Breathe like your Life depends on It
Surya Yoga (out of print)
The Yoga of Purification and Transformation

About the Author

Rudra Shivananda is dedicated to the service of humanity through the furthering of human awareness and spiritual evolution. He teaches that the only lasting way to bring happiness into one's life is by a consistent practice of awareness and transformation.

Rudra Shivananda is committed to spreading the message of the immortal Being called *Babaji*. He teaches the message of World and Individual Peace through the practice of *Kriya Yoga*. A student and teacher of Yoga for more than 30 years, he is initiated by his Master Yogiraj Gurunath Siddhanath as an *Acharya* or Spiritual Preceptor in Kriya Yoga and the Indian *Nath* Tradition, closely associated with the *Siddha* tradition. He is also experienced as a *Shakti* Healer and Astrologer with expertise in the healing and spiritual uses of mantras, gemstones and essential oils. He lives and works in the San Francisco Bay area, and has given initiations and workshops in USA, Ireland, India, England Spain, Russia, Brazil, Japan and Australia.

CPSIA information can be obtained
at www.ICGtesting.com
Printed in the USA
BVOW03s1620211117
501000BV00002B/259/P